George Putnam Upton

Woman in Music

Second Edition

George Putnam Upton

Woman in Music
Second Edition

ISBN/EAN: 9783337085391

Printed in Europe, USA, Canada, Australia, Japan

Cover: Foto ©Thomas Meinert / pixelio.de

More available books at **www.hansebooks.com**

WOMAN IN MUSIC

BY

GEORGE P. UPTON
AUTHOR OF "THE STANDARD OPERAS," ETC., ETC.

Second Edition
REVISED AND ENLARGED

CHICAGO
A. C. McCLURG AND COMPANY
1886

As a Tribute

TO THE

FRIENDSHIP OF A STEADFAST COMRADE,

AND AS AN ACKNOWLEDGMENT OF HER
HELPFUL SERVICE,

I Dedicate

THESE STUDIES OF MY LEISURE HOURS

TO MY WIFE.

PREFACE.

THE first edition of this work appeared in 1880; but its circulation was interrupted by a fire which destroyed the plates. A renewed demand for the work seems, however, to warrant the author in presenting a revised and much enlarged edition, in which the scope of the general subject has been widened, and its illustration has been made still more complete by additional stories of composers whose success has been due in some degree to the influence of woman. The work has been written in the leisure hours of other pursuits, and of necessity is compiled from the writer's musical readings. A long list of authorities has been consulted for facts bearing upon the subject; and, so far as is known to the writer, only the highest have been laid under contribution. As a well-stocked musical library is something of a rarity in this country, he ventures to hope that his compilations, and his comments thereon, will be of interest to the musical student, and possibly of value to the general public.

G. P. U.

Chicago, 1886.

IF to the depths of tenderness and devotion in which the true and irresistible empire of woman must commence, and deprived of which she is only an enigma without a possible solution, Nature should unite the most brilliant gifts of genius, the miraculous spectacle of the Greek Fire would be renewed; the glittering flames would again sport over the abysses of the ocean without being extinguished or submerged in the chilling depths, adding, as the living hues were thrown upon the surging waves, the glowing dyes of the purple fire to the celestial blue of the heaven-reflecting sea. — LISZT.

THERE is no living soul so capable of enjoying and correctly judging of a work of art as a finely cultivated woman; for her whole inner life is in itself a sort of work of art. Even the highest kind of men have something formless and unfinished about their natures. The hasty demands of life do not stop to inquire whether it be Sabbath or not : they surprise man amid the worship of the beautiful, and scarcely give him time to refrain from profanation of the altar. But the life of woman, — how calm as a festival day, how full of harmony may it not, should it not be! When the storm-bells of passion have rung out, then a pure ether remains behind. . . . In such minds the impression made by a work of art is correct and immediate ; for they are prepared to receive it, — themselves serene and pure as bridal devotion. — EHLERT.

CONTENTS.

PART I.
	PAGE
WOMAN IN MUSIC	15

PART II.
JOHANN SEBASTIAN BACH	35
GEORGE FREDERICK HÄNDEL	48
LUDWIG VAN BEETHOVEN	60
FRANCIS JOSEPH HAYDN	84
WOLFGANG AMADEUS MOZART	96
FRANZ SCHUBERT	112
ROBERT SCHUMANN	125
FELIX MENDELSSOHN BARTHOLDY	138
FREDERICK CHOPIN	149
CARL MARIA VON WEBER	162
RICHARD WAGNER	177

PART III.
WOMAN AS THE INTERPRETER OF MUSIC	187
APPENDIX	209
DEDICATIONS	210
INDEX	219

PART I.

WOMAN IN MUSIC.

JOHANN SEBASTIAN BACH.

I, my Fabius, who am in other respects an admirer of antiquity, am of opinion that my Bach, and others like him, unite in their own persons many Orpheuses and twenty Arions. — GESNER.

TO thoroughly appreciate the influence of woman upon Sebastian Bach in his musical development and creations, it is necessary to regard the modest and God-fearing cantor of St. Thomas not only as a musician but also as a man. He has left an imperishable name, and his musical creations are the very foundations of the art; and yet his life was mainly spent within the family circle, where, in the true patriarchal spirit, he ruled over his numerous progeny. This domestic characteristic distinguished all the Bachs, from the time when Veit Bach, the old baker who played his zither while his mill was running, and the founder of the family, travelled into Thuringia from Hungary, that he might be free to worship God as he pleased. They were all musicians; and their love of music, as well as their remarkable purity of sentiment and strength of family affection, bound them closely together. At one time there were no less than thirty Bachs who were organists in Thuringia, Franconia, and Saxony. Nothing is more beautiful in the records of music than their anniversary meetings, upon which occasions they gathered together from all parts of Germany, and enjoyed a genuine feast of music in singing chorals and folk-songs, and improvising. No jar or disagreement ever disturbed these meetings. They were as calm and peaceful as the movement of the chorals which opened and closed them. They were simple, unaffected, pious people, remarkably gifted in musical knowledge, — in fact, renowned all over Germany for their skill, — and yet to a large extent living within themselves, and depending upon their homes for their enjoyment.

Of this constellation, Johann Sebastian Bach was the very sun and centre. He seems to have had none of the contrarieties or eccentricities which have characterized so many other musical geniuses. His mother died shortly after he was born, and his father when the boy was but ten years of age. His youth was spent in the home of his elder brother, Johann Christoph, an organist and music-master, who brought him up with an austerity of discipline which seems very harsh, and which particularly manifested itself, for some unaccountable reason, in the apparent determination to crush out his musical impulses and ambitions. His severe training, however, gave him self-reliance. He grew up to be a self-sustained, evenly poised man, simple and unostentatious in his bearing, strictly honorable in his intercourse with men, strong and unvarying in his home love, and guided in every event of life by a strict morality born of sincere religion. The spot where Luther translated the Bible into German overlooked his native place, and on the same spot the minnesingers had fought their romantic battles of song; and the religion of the one and the romance of the other affected his life until its close. He was an affectionate father, laboring manfully and incessantly to support his large family; a good citizen, faithfully fulfilling all his duties and commanding universal respect; a plain, humble man, despising rank and show, making no boast of his grand achievements, and yet recognized in the court of Frederick the Great as above courtiers and nobility, by the title of his genius.

Such a man, domestic by nature, spending most of his time and doing most of his work at home, and, more than all, doing this work for what seems now a beggarly pittance, needed for a companion a sensible, practical, industrious, and economical woman, capable of administering the affairs of the family in such manner that his musical labor, which was incessant, might not be disturbed by household cares, or solicitude as to the ability of the lean family purse to meet the demands upon it. Such a woman he found in his cousin Maria Barbara Bach, the youngest daughter of Johann Michael Bach, of Gehren, himself a composer of no mean ability. He made her acquaintance in Arnstadt, where he was appointed first organist of the new church in 1703. He was at that time too poor to marry; but the attachment between them was so strong that they mutually agreed to wait until a position lucrative enough to support them should offer itself. They did not have to wait long. In 1706 he was successful in obtaining the position of organist of

St. Blasius Church, at Mühlhausen, and was left free to fix his own salary. Although upon the verge of marriage, the contract made with the town authorities shows that his requirements for establishing a family and founding a home were modest in the extreme. The contract reads: " Eighty-five guldens (a little more than thirty-five dollars), three malters of corn, two clafters of wood (one of beech and one of other wood), and six schock of small firewood, to be brought to his door." He also requests that he may be helped "with the loan of a cart in bringing his furniture from Arnstadt." He assumed his duties at Mühlhausen in 1707; and in October of that year he and Maria Barbara were married, starting in life with the modest outfit already mentioned. Very little is known of her, except that she was an affectionate and dutiful wife, of even temper and sunny disposition, contented with her lot, and so prudent and thrifty in her management that the home of Johann Sebastian was always a happy one, and his musical labors were never disturbed by the interposition of household troubles and annoyances. She died in 1720, during Bach's absence at Carlsbad with Prince Leopold, and so suddenly that no news of it reached him until after she was buried. She bore him eight children, five sons and three daughters, — Caroline Dorothea, born in 1708; Wilhelm Friedemann, born in 1710, died at Berlin in 1784; Carl Philipp Emanuel, born in 1714, and commonly known as the "Berlin Bach," who died at Hamburg in 1788; Johann Gottfried Bernhard, born in 1715; and Leopold August, born in 1718. In addition to these, there were a pair of twins, who died before they were a year old; and a daughter, who died very young.

There is no record to show that his first wife was a musician, or that she had musical taste or feeling; but it is on record that the thirteen years of hard labor and of incessant struggle with the necessities of life were years of mutual happiness, respect, and affection. She was thrifty, contented, industrious, and withal unselfish, — qualities which are very essential to happiness in life on an income of less than fifty dollars a year and perquisites of the most meagre description. We may therefore conclude that Sebastian Bach sincerely mourned the loss of the companion so suddenly snatched away from him. His situation in life was such, however, that he could not sorrow long. The necessities of constant labor, the daily recurrence of multifarious household duties, and the pressing cares of his little flock of children, all appealed to him to supply the place of her who had gone, so that he might be relieved of these exacting and worrying household cares, and give his sole attention to his art. A year and a half after her death, in the year 1721, he married Anna Magdalena Wülkens, the youngest daughter of a trumpeter, court musician to the Duke of Weissenfeld. He was then thirty-six years of age, and she was fifteen years his junior. This disparity of years, however, never threw a shadow upon the affections of the two, which remained beautiful and undisturbed until his death. The union was a perfect one, perhaps more perfect than the first; for, in addition to her devotion to household duties and her prudent and economical management of their little income, she was a musician of exceptional talent and had a very fine voice. His income, although larger than he had received heretofore, was still small; for two years after his marriage, when he signed his contracts as cantor of St. Thomas, at Leipzig, his yearly stipend was eighty-seven thalers and twelve groschen (about sixty-five dollars); sixteen scheffel of corn; thirteen thalers, three groschen, for wood and candles; one thaler, eight groschen, interest on a legacy; lodging and firewood free. This sum, with certain fees for services at marriages and funerals, was his only recompense for the arduous labors at the St. Thomas School, and the equally arduous labor of composing and conducting the music for four churches. Under her prudent management, however, they lived very comfortably; and a new element of happiness sprang up in his home, growing out of her knowledge and love of music. She had a soprano voice of beautiful quality, and a knowledge of the technique of music of such a decided character that for five years after her marriage she and the children studied with Bach in thorough-bass and piano music; the father finding time in the midst of his many duties to give them the benefits of his knowledge. He wrote out for her the rules of thorough-bass; and there still exists a testimonial of his great interest in her musical progress in the collection of "easy pieces for the piano," written in 1722, and inscribed with the autograph, "Clavier Büchlein vor Anna Magdalena Bach." Three years later he had completed for her a whole volume of music, containing forty-six preludes, minuets, rondos, polonaises, etc., thirty-five of which are for the piano; among them the favorite C major prelude, No. 1 of the "Wohltemperirte Clavier;" five chorals, — "Wer nur den lieben Gott lässt walten," "Gieb dich zufrieden," "Schaff's mit mir Gott," "Dir, Jehovah, will ich singen," and "O Ewigkeit, Du Donnerwort;" and, lastly, seven songs, followed by a wedding poem, which are not only of peculiar interest because they were written for his wife, but also because they are the only short songs, not of a sacred character, which Bach has left. To these songs Bach probably furnished words as well as music; and one of them, the "Willst du dein Herz mir schenken," was inspired by his love for her in the days of their brief courtship. Nearly all of them are filled with true and tender devotion, none more so than that which asks the question so happily answered by a lifetime of love, — the song of their courtship, which brought them together in a bond of love too strong for anything but death to sever. In this volume, written in figured basses, her own handiwork appears, where she has filled in the chords; and his corrections scattered through them leave an interesting and touching souvenir of the great master, and the pupil who was to him the nearest and dearest of all.

Bach died on the 28th of July, 1750, after long and keen suffering, during the midst of which he did not cease work. Only a short time before his death, he dictated his last work, "Wenn wir in höchsten Nöthen sein,"—a choral born of his suffering and inspired by his religion, a touching reflex of his own pitiable condition. He died in his sleep, and no stone marks the spot in the Leipzig churchyard where his body rests. The only record which is left is to be found in the register of deaths, which thus affirms: "A man, age 67, M. Johann Sebastian Bach, Musical Director and Singing-Master at the St. Thomas School, was carried to his grave in the hearse, July 30, 1750." His widow survived him seven years, supporting herself as she best could upon the scanty pension granted to cantors, and by the sale of her husband's manuscripts. She bore him thirteen children, but six of whom survived their father's death,—among them, Johann Christoph Friedrich, born in 1732, known as the "Bückeburger Bach;" and Johann Christian, born in 1735, who became famous as the "London Bach." Only one daughter, Regina Susanna, survived the mother, whose extreme poverty aroused a widespread feeling of compassion, which took the form of a public contribution in 1801, and becomes more than usually interesting, as it allies the name of Beethoven with that of Bach. On the 19th of May, 1801, Friedrich Rochlitz, one of Bach's most zealous admirers, and the editor of the Leipzig " Allgemeine Musikzeitung," writes : —

" Our appeal for the support of the only survivor of the Bach family, Sebastian Bach's youngest daughter, has not been overlooked by the public. . . . With deep emotion we received on the 10th of May, through the Viennese musician, Herr Andreas Streicher, the considerable sum of 307 Viennese florins, exchanged by the banker Löhr of this city for 200 Reichthaler from the undersigned persons.

" The collection was made by the musician above mentioned, with the assistance of Count Fries in Vienna. . . . At the same time the celebrated Viennese composer and pianist, Herr von Beethoven, volunteered to publish one of his newest works, through Messrs. Breitkopf and Härtel, for the sole benefit of Bach's daughter, that the good old woman might from time to time derive benefits from it, at the same time using all his efforts for the most speedy publication possible, that she may not perchance die before this object is attained."

Destiny ordered kindly for Sebastian Bach in the arrangement of his domestic life with reference to his musical creations. Notwithstanding his immense and incessant labors, especially in connection with the St. Thomas School and the Leipzig churches, the cares and troubles naturally created by such a large family of children, and the small compensation received for his work, his life ran smoothly, and the grand monument he was erecting for posterity never suffered either in its fair proportions or its complete form. At the outset of his career, and before he entered upon the really great work of his life, he needed for a companion a thrifty, prudent woman, of even disposition and contented nature; and such a one he found in his cousin Maria Barbara. After her death, and when his name had begun to be known as a great organist and composer beyond mere local limits, he still needed a thrifty and prudent and even-tempered woman, but, still more than this, a woman who could sympathize with him, and encourage, assist, and inspire him in his musical labors; and such a one he found in Anna Magdalena. There can be no doubt that the second marriage was the happier, although she was the wife of his prime, and the romance of youth had faded away before the realities of life, with so many of which Bach had to contend. How great that inspiration was his music shows. It is doubly inscribed. First, like Haydn, he wrote upon his scores his reverence to God,— S. D. G. (*Soli Deo Gloria*), — and then his love for his wife.

GEORGE FREDERICK HÄNDEL.

Remember Händel! who that was not born
Deaf as the dead to harmony, forgets,
Or can, the more than Homer of his age?
                                        COWPER.

IT is said by all his biographers that Händel was never a victim of the tender passion, though many ladies paid homage to his genius by laying siege to his heart. There was one love, however, in the manifestation of which he was both ardent and constant; that was his love for his mother. Händel's father, George, had studied the rude surgery of the time, with Christoph Oettinger, the town barber of Halle, and eventually married his widow, Frau Anna Oettinger, Feb. 20, 1643, and continued the business of his employer. Frau Anna gave birth to six children, and died in 1682, at the advanced age of seventy-two. In less than six months the bereaved husband contracted a second marriage with Dorothea, daughter of Pastor Taust, of Giebichenstein, who is described by Rochstro as "a lady equally respected for the gentleness of her demeanor, her loving submission to parental and conjugal authority, her earnest piety, and her reverence for, and intimate acquaintance with, the text and teaching of the Holy Scriptures, — qualities which were all faithfully reproduced in the character of her children." These children were a son who died at birth; two daughters, Dorothea Sophie and Johanna Christiana; and George Frederick, the subject of this sketch. Although the family was not an artistic one in any sense, — indeed, the father was so averse to music that he declared he would have no such "jingling" in the house, — his childhood was a happy one. The old surgeon was resolutely bent upon making a lawyer of his son; but as usual the maternal instincts apprehended the true bent of the boy's passion, and we may well imagine that she found more than one way to encourage him, in spite of the father's opposition. The same authority quoted above says he was "the fondest hope of a mother, to whose tender solicitude he owed the training which, through all the trials and vicissitudes of a long and more than ordinarily eventful life, kept him honest and just and true, and secured him the respect of princes, and the affection of all who were not blinded by jealousy to the splendor of his genius and the depth of his moral worth." She superintended his education, and prepared him for his life-struggle with tender devotion, even stinting herself, after his father's death, to provide him with the means of continuing his musical studies. Although it has been said of him, by some of the earlier biographers, that his social affections were not very strong, he was not lacking in filial piety. In June, 1725, he writes a very cordial letter from London to his brother-in-law at Halle, expressing his deep regret that he cannot spare time to visit his mother. " I cannot be so ungrateful," he says, " as to pass over in silence the goodness you have shown to my mother in her advanced age, for which I offer you my very humble thanks. You know how deeply I am interested in all that concerns her, and can therefore judge the depth of the obligation under which you have placed me." He was always loyal in his affection for her, and in his numerous journeys never failed to find time to visit her. While in Venice in 1729, he received a letter from his brother-in-law, informing him that his mother had been seized with a paralytic attack. He hurried to Halle with all possible despatch, and found her sufficiently recovered to be able to walk about, though she had lost her sight and could only recognize him by the pressure of the hand. The meeting was a very sorrowful one to both, though mutual love lightened the pain. A year afterward she died suddenly, while Händel was in London; and in the funeral oration delivered over her grave, this love which had so strongly affected their lives was particularly dwelt upon. In his reply to the letter informing him of her death, Händel gives still another evidence of his great love for the mother to whom he owed so much. He says:—

"I cannot yet restrain my tears. But it has pleased the Most High to enable me to submit with Christian calmness to his holy will. Your thoughtfulness will never pass from my remembrance until, after this life, we are once more united, which may the All-good God in his mercy grant us!"

The loving mother prepared him for his career, and upon its very threshold he again experienced the beneficence of woman's influence. Friedrich, the Elector of Brandenburg, afterward King Friedrich I. of Prussia, was a generous patron of arts. His consort, the Electress Sophie Charlotte, who was subsequently styled the "Philosophic Queen," was not only a warm friend of artists, but was herself one of the most accomplished musicians in Europe, and more than once occupied the conductor's desk in concerts and at operatic performances. The Electoral palace was the favorite resort of artists from all parts of Europe, and thither Händel was sent as a child. He was most kindly received by the Electress. She was delighted with his performances, introduced him to prominent artists who gave him many valuable hints, — among them, Ariosti and Buononcini, — and at last offered to take him into the service of the Court, send him free of expense to Italy to complete his education, and upon his return to give him an important position. His father, however, declined the offer. Hamburg meanwhile was rapidly competing with Berlin as an art centre; and after the death of the generous Electress, thither went Händel to continue his studies.

About this time an odd experience befell him, and all the more comical when his aversion to matrimony is considered. Buxtehude, the veteran organist at Lübeck, was about to retire from his position, and the place was offered for competition. Händel, in company with Mattheson, the principal tenor of the Hamburg Theatre, went to Lübeck to compete for it. Mattheson himself relates their experiences : —

"We played on almost every organ and harpsichord in the place, and with regard to our performances, agreed between ourselves that he should play only upon the organ and I upon the harpsichord. We listened also to the veteran performer, in the Marienkirche, with deep attention. But because the question of succession involved also that of a marriage contract, into which we neither of us had the slightest desire to enter, we left the place, after receiving many compliments, unusual honors, and very pleasant entertainment. Johann Christian Schieferdecker afterward brought the affair to a more satisfactory conclusion : accepted the bride, after the death of her father, Buxtehude, in 1707, and obtained the coveted appointment."

The royal ladies of the English Court were the devoted friends of Händel. He had a handsome pension from the bounty of Queen

Anne. When George I. succeeded to the throne, he and the royal family were regular attendants at the theatre whenever his operas were given. Eventually the King added a second pension of £200 a year, and appointed him music-master to the daughters of the Prince of Wales, afterward George II., which brought him a third pension of £200 from the private purse of the Princess, afterward Queen Caroline. Her death, in 1737, deprived him of one of his most devoted friends. How deeply he was attached to her is evidenced by the exquisitely beautiful anthem he wrote for her funeral, "The Ways of Zion do mourn." He gave lessons to all the children of the royal family. The Princess Anne was devotedly attached to him; and when she left England, her last act of kindness to him was to commend him to the favor of Lord Harvey, a favorite of the Queen. This royal favor must have been particularly grateful to him, as it was bestowed at a time when his Italian rivals were organizing cabals against him and seeking in every way to undermine and ruin him. And yet, indebted as he was to them, he never restrained his temper when they violated the proprieties. Schoelcher relates the following incident:—

"At the concerts which he conducted for Frederick, Prince of Wales, if the Prince and his wife were not punctual to the stated time, we are told that the conductor used to be very violent; and the son of George II. — to his great honor be it said — respected him too much to be offended. If the ladies of the Princess talked instead of listening, his rage was uncontrollable, and sometimes carried him to the length of swearing and calling names, even in the presence of royalty; whereupon the gentle Princess, who loved him much, would say to the talkative ones: 'Hush! hush! Händel is in a passion.'"

Another instance of his terrible temper is related by Rochstro: —

"At the first rehearsal of 'Ottone,' Francesca Cuzzoni flatly refused to sing the lovely aria 'Falsa immagine,' which Händel had written expressly for her. Said Händel: 'I know, Madame, that you are a very devil, but I will let you see that I am Beelzebub, the prince of devils;' and with that he seized her in his arms and threatened to throw her out of the window, whereupon she yielded in terror to his superior will, sang the song in exact accordance with his directions, and achieved in it one of her most brilliant triumphs."

In view of his success with refractory songstresses, one is disposed to wish that the conductors of our own time had an equally healthy discipline in the ranks of their capricious and moody *prime donne.*

Händel, as has already been said, was averse to matrimony. More than this, he was not very social by nature and not at all domestic in his habits. His complete devotion to his art, his impatience with whatever crossed him, his hot temper, and the peculiar idiosyncrasies of his nature illy fitted him to make any woman happy ; hence it was fortunate that he was never in love with any of the sex except his mother. In his long and eventful career he was constantly associated with ladies, and was much admired by them ; but none of them touched his heart. It is said by his biographers that he spent many of his afternoons at the organ of St. Paul's, in the midst of his admirers, and at night resorted to the Queen's Arms, a tavern near by, where he played the harpsichord, smoked his pipe, and drank his beer. As he became more absorbed in his compositions he cut loose from all society, and only associated with three intimate friends, not one of whom had musical tastes. His chief amusement was to visit exhibitions of pictures. Hawkins says of him : —

" His social affections were not very strong, and to this it may be imputed that he spent his whole life in celibacy. No impertinent visits and few engagements to parties of pleasure were suffered to interrupt the course of his studies."

He had no passion except for music, and yet the opportunities for the exercise of the all-engrossing passion were not lacking. While he was in Italy, being then in his twenty-fourth year, the Prince of Tuscany, brother of the Grand Duke John Gaston de Médicis, was present at performances of his operas "Almeria" and "Florinda," and was so delighted with them that he gave him an invitation to go to Florence. When the opportunity came he went there and brought out the opera of "Roderigo," written for the occasion, for which he was honored by the Grand Duke with a present in money and a service of plate. It was often the custom at that day for the ladies of the Courts to sing in the works produced in the royal presence; and upon this occasion the Archduchess Vittoria, a beautiful woman, took the principal rôle. Burney describes her as "a songstress of great talent." She conceived so violent a passion for him that she even followed him from Florence to Venice, and literally demanded that he should marry her, after he had manifested a repugnance to her approaches. The choleric

Händel, however, repelled her suit with disdain, and she gave up the chase. His decision, or rather his indifference, fortunately saved him from disastrous consequences, as the lady who had been so importunate was the mistress of the Prince who had invited him to Florence.

The author of the " Anecdotes of Händel " also relates the following incidents, in which he was a party of the second part: —

"When he was young, two of his scholars, ladies of considerable fortune, were so much enamoured of him that each was desirous of a matrimonial alliance. The first is said to have fallen a victim to her attachment. Händel would have married her, but his pride was stung by the coarse declaration of her mother, that she never would consent to the marriage of her daughter with a fiddler; and, indignant at the expression, he declined all further intercourse. After the death of the mother the father renewed the acquaintance, and informed him that all obstacles were removed, but he replied that the time was now past; and the young lady fell into a decline, which soon terminated her existence. The second attachment was a lady splendidly related, whose hand he might have obtained by renouncing his profession. That condition he resolutely refused, and laudably declined the connection which was to prove a restriction on the great faculties of his mind."

It may be remarked that the first story does not comport with the well-known character of Händel, and as it is not mentioned in any of his biographies, may be set down as one of those popular romances which attach to the careers of all geniuses. The second, however, is characteristic of him, though it is to be regretted that the details of his refusal are not given. It would be refreshing to know what the irascible composer would have said to the proposition that he should exchange his music for a wife. No woman touched him so nearly as to affect his music; and yet, without his mother's warm affection and sympathy for him in his unartistic home, and her determination that he should follow the course he had marked out for himself, he would have lost many of his early advantages. Had it not been also for the devoted friendship and generous support of good Queen Caroline and the princesses of her Court, he would have fared badly, in England, at the hands of his Italian rivals.

LUDWIG VAN BEETHOVEN.

He lived in the ideal world which Petrarch and Dante described, and his passion took nothing from his austerity. Unable to marry, he remained chaste; and he loved as purely as he wrote. He hated licentious speech, and blamed the "Don Giovanni" of Mozart, because a thing so holy as art should not so prostitute itself as to serve to link together so scandalous a story. — M. TAINE.

LENZ says in one of his rhapsodies: "In the arts the animating or life-giving element is furnished by the sentiment of love." In music it finds its highest and truest expression, and in no music more clearly than in the immortal works of Beethoven. No other creation in tones has done so much to dignify and ennoble love as his one opera, "Fidelio;" no song has so expressed its beauty and its ardor as that most perfect amatory lyric, the "Adelaide." If the passion of love which is pictured in these two works and in nearly all the others which he created, whether song, sonata, or symphony, and the ardent aspiration as well as profound self-abasement of religion which characterize the Second Mass and clothe its measures with the divine presence, had been wanting in his life, it is almost unquestionable that he would have yielded in the bitter struggle with adverse circumstances, and that he would not remain to-day as the one composer to whom all the world does homage. No musician has ever so completely imbued his music with feeling, — that feeling which implies sympathy with passion in all its heights and depths, with the inner life of humanity, with the noblest forms of emotion in man, and with the grandest aspects of Nature, — that feeling which could not have existed without this great underlying principle of love, joined with a naturally reverential and devotional habit of being.

Beethoven's life was a battle with circumstances, commenced in his boyhood, ending only on his death-bed, and fitly typified by the fearful thunders and lightnings of the storm that raged about him in his last moments. The dissipations of his father, a drunken musician, cast a gloom over his earlier life. The drudgery and the misery of his home fostered a misanthropic feeling. The want of general and liberal culture which he might have had under more favorable circumstances annoyed him all through life. In the midst of the corrupt society of Vienna he had led a blameless career; but even this could not save him from feeling the wretched effects of this corruption in his own family. His nephew Karl was left to his care by his father; but to secure the boy, whom he loved as if he were his son, he had to prove that the mother was a dissolute woman. He abandoned his bachelor habits, and commenced housekeeping on the boy's account; he hoarded up his money to educate him; he lavished his affection upon him; and the graceless wretch requited it all by the most infamous career of dissipation, making the uncle all the more suspicious and misanthropic. From this point on, the story is one of the most pitiful kind. Painful physical troubles set in one after the other, the most painful being his deafness, which so increased upon him that in the latter years of his life, during which he produced his greatest works,

— the Mass in D, the Choral Symphony, and the last sonatas and quartets, — he could hear nothing. "*Miser et pauper sum*," he writes in his journal at this time. Over his sonata for violoncello, Op. 59, he writes, "*Inter lacrymas et luctum*." Where in all history is there a sadder wail of despair, a more pitiable outburst of grief, than is to be found in his utterance : " I have drunk to the dregs a cup of bitter sorrow, and already earned martyrdom in art"? or in this extract from a letter to his friend Wegeler : —

" How often have I cursed my existence! Plutarch has led me to resignation. I will, if possible, set fate at defiance, although there must be moments in my life when I shall be the most unhappy of God's creatures. I entreat you to say nothing of my affliction to any one, not even to Lorchen. . . . Resignation ! what a miserable refuge! and yet it is my sole remaining one."

In the midst of this life, in which this musical colossus was not only struggling with painful physical ailments and severe mental troubles, but was also annoyed with a swarm of petty household discomforts brought upon himself by his love for his worthless nephew, there are episodes upon which it is pleasant to dwell, growing out of his relations to the other sex, of whom, most unquestionably, he was a passionate though very diffusive admirer; and just as his inner life developed more and more grandly, as his deafness compelled him to retire within himself, and gave birth to his most sublime creations, so the influence of woman, previous to this time, had aroused in him a wonderful sense of beauty and depth of tenderness, which were helping to prepare the way for the more majestic and enduring works which were to crown the close of his remarkable career.

Beethoven's earliest attachment was to the Breuning family in Bonn, who were held in the highest esteem in that city. They were among his earliest friends and protectors, and they clove to him to the last. Frau von Breuning took a deep interest in him, and he regarded her in the sacred light of a mother. Her son Stephen was one of his warmest friends; likewise Eleanore, the daughter, who subsequently married Dr. Wegeler, then his friend, and after his death his biographer. Some writers, more particularly those of the Rau and "Furioso" class, who have rhapsodized over the memory of a man in whose life there was not a trace of romance, have sought to make it appear that Eleanore was Beethoven's first love; but there is nothing in his relations to her, or in his correspondence with her or with the family, that indicates any sentiment on his part except that of warm and exalted friendship. After a year's absence from the family, during which there had been an estrangement between them, he writes to Eleanore from Vienna (Nov. 2, 1793) : —

"Little as I may deserve favor in your eyes, believe me, my dear *friend* (let me still call you so), I have suffered and still suffer severely from the privation of your friendship. Never can I forget you and your dear mother."

And with this letter he sends her, as a souvenir, his variations upon the "Se vuol ballare" of Mozart. Nothing more ardent than expressions of this kind appear in any of his letters to her. It was in the Breuning house that he always found shelter from the misery and squalor of his own home. It was through this family that he first made acquaintance with German literature and the poets, whose creations he so often set to music, and whose lofty and majestic spirit is so clearly reflected in his larger works. All the members of the family were musical, Frau von Breuning not the least so; and it was her strong influence that kept him at work, and directed his genius in the highest and best ways. She understood his eccentric moods, and could make allowance for them. She knew when to urge him on to his best endeavor, how to encourage him, and how to manage his restless, wayward, and gloomy disposition. This woman, more than all others, helped to lay the broad and strong foundation upon which Beethoven's fame now rests; and to her, more than to any other, should be due the credit for the lofty position he holds in the world of music. He came to her as a son would come to his mother for aid and counsel; and she, better than all others, understood him. She foresaw his future, because she recognized his genius; and she not only urged him on to the accomplishment of its mission, but she helped to direct it in the right course by supplying it with the noblest and most dignified examples of art for study.

While there was no more ardent feeling than that of friendship in the breast of Beethoven towards the Breuning family, there came one day into the circle a friend of Eleanore's who aroused the first manifestation of love on his part. It was a sudden flame, suddenly extinguished. The friend was Jeannette d'Honrath, a young lady of Cologne, who was a frequent visitor at the Breuning house, a beautiful blonde, a person of amiable disposition, a good singer, and a confirmed coquette withal. She bestowed her favor so equally between Beethoven and Stephen Breuning, and yet so deftly, that each believed himself to be an accepted lover. She laid sportive siege to the infatuated Beethoven with a well-known song of that day, —

> "What! part with thee this very day?
> My heart a thousand times says, Nay!"

And when he was away, the same song did good service for Stephen. Thus each victim was enmeshed in the fair singer's toils, unknown to the other; and it was not until she had flitted away, with much feigned regret, that the two luckless suitors discovered she was affianced all this time to a young Austrian officer, Major Greth, whom she afterward married, and who subsequently rose to the rank of general. The fair Jeannette and her gallant husband passed away in due time, and, like many other nobodies, have come down to posterity by virtue of some slight connection with Beethoven. It is to be presumed that neither Ludwig nor Stephen brooded long over their slight at the hands of the Cologne beauty, since we find them not long afterward paying assiduous court in the train of suitors and admirers that thronged about Barbara Koch, the beauty of Bonn. Her mother, a widow, kept a coffee-house which was the favorite resort of professors and students. The fair Barbara herself was a very cultivated person, and she drew about her those of like character; and in the pleasant evenings at the coffee-house, art, philosophy, and music were discussed, all having a direct bearing upon the future development of the young musician. There is nothing to indicate that the acquaintance left any lasting impression upon him; though he corresponded with her after he had left Bonn, as we find, in a letter to Eleanore von Breuning, who was her friend, his complaint that he had written twice to Barbara and she had not answered, which may be accounted for by her marriage not long after to Count Anton von Belderbusch, in whose family she had previously served as governess.

Wegeler, his biographer, says of him, "Beethoven war immer in Liebesverhältnissen;" and he himself said that he once loved the same woman for seven whole months, — not a flippant remark, as would seem at the first glance, but indicating a mood of his being which may well be described in his own words : —

" I was born with a passionate and excitable temperament; I am keenly susceptible to the pleasures of society ; my heart and mind were, even from childhood, prone to the most tender feelings of affection."

With such a temperament, one may well fancy that the list of his attachments was a long one ; though the most of them were by no means serious, since it was his fate as a rule to bestow them upon ladies whose rank forbade any possibility of requital. These must be passed over lightly, though in the case of some there is a degree of interest attaching to them that warrants a detailed consideration. They were nearly all his pupils. Among them was Mlle. de Gerardi, of whom we know very little, who laid siege to the susceptible Beethoven in verse, but without any more practical result than, as he says in a letter, his serious annoyance. The young Baroness von Drossdich, a somewhat volatile and eccentric person whom he addresses in his letters as " My esteemed Thérèse," was a favorite with him. In a letter written in 1809, he urges her not to forget her music, and mentions sending her several of his compositions. Upon one occasion he paid her a visit at Mödling, and, not finding her at home, tore a sheet of music-paper from a book, wrote upon it some music for her, set to a verse of Matthisson's, and on the reverse dedicated it "To my dear Thérèse." The close of the letter to which I have referred clearly shows the strength of his regard for her: —

"Farewell, my esteemed Thérèse. I wish you all the good and charm that life can offer. Think of me kindly, and forget my follies. Rest assured that no one would more rejoice to hear of your happiness, even were you to feel no interest in your devoted servant and friend."

After his rupture with Thérèse, another intimate affection consoled him for her absence. In 1811 his pecuniary troubles and physical ailments influenced him to quit Vienna for a time. His first thought was to go to Italy; but by the advice of his physicians he changed his intentions, and selected Teplitz, the little Bohemian town, where two years later the King of Prussia and the Emperors of Austria and Russia signed the treaty of the Holy Alliance. It was always a favorite resort with artists and the aristocracy. In the select society to which he had the *entrée* he met many old acquaintances and made some new ones, — among them, the poet Tiedge. There was one, however, who made a deeper impression than all the rest. It was Amelia de Sebald, a young and beautiful concert-singer, who cultivated music as an amateur, but had, it is said, a very sympathetic voice and genuine talent. When the fair singer left Teplitz, the master first became aware of the real impression she had made upon him, and in a letter to Tiedge he thus unbosoms himself: —

" Two affectionate words for a farewell would have sufficed me ; alas ! not even one was said to me ! The Countess von der Recke sends me a pressure of the hand ; it is something, and I kiss her hands as a token of gratitude ; but Amelia has not even saluted me. Every day I am angry at myself in not having profited by her sojourn at Teplitz, seeking her companionship sooner. It is a frightful thing to make the acquaintance of such a sweet creature, and to lose her immediately ; and nothing is more insupportable than thus to have to confess one's own foolishness. I propose to remain here until the end of the month of September. Write me as to how long you reckon to remain in Dresden ; it is not impossible that I may take a run to the Saxon metropolis. . . . Be happy, if suffering humanity can be. Give, on my part, to the

Countess a cordial but respectful pressure of the hand, and to Amelia a tender kiss — if nobody there can see."

The next year Beethoven again visited Teplitz, with the hope of seeing her; but the fair vision had vanished. His only consolation, if consolation it can be called, was the opportunity it gave him of making the acquaintance of Goethe. Except in so far as this acquaintance led to the friendship between himself and the wonderful child Bettina, of which more hereafter, his relations to the great poet were of no special value to him. Goethe had too little music in his composition to appreciate him at his true value, and he was too much of a king-worshipper to suit such a red republican as Beethoven.

The Baroness Dorothea Van Ertmann was another titled pupil whom he held in affectionate esteem, who inspired his wonderful sonata, Op. 101, and who was afterward a warm friend of Mendelssohn. She was the wife of an Austrian captain at eighteen, who died subsequently as a field-marshal at Milan. She commenced her musical studies at a very early age, and made the acquaintance of Beethoven by chance, while playing some of his sonatas for the first time. He accidentally overheard her, and was so captivated with her style that he offered to teach her, and soon became a daily visitor at her house. As a teacher he was severe with her; as a friend, affectionate; and when she had lost the last of her children, he shared her grief and gave expression to it by extemporizing upon the piano in her apartments for her. It is said that when he ended his fantasie, her eyes were filled with tears so that she could not speak to him. Among others who captivated him during his orchestral career in Bonn, was a fair and brilliant singer, Magdalena Willmann, filling at that time an engagement in the Court Opera at Vienna, to whom, it is intimated, he offered his hand in marriage. It would appear that his offer was a serious one; but the repulse was prompt and merciless, the great songstress, afterward Mrs. Galvani, declaring that she rejected him because he was "so ugly and half cracked."

Mlle. Marie Koschak, who subsequently married Dr. Pachler, an advocate in Gratz, a very beautiful woman, and an amateur musician of extraordinary merit, inspired in Beethoven a glow warmer than that of friendship, or even affection. In one of his letters he writes: —

"Love alone, yes, love alone, can make your life happier. O God! grant that I may at last find her who can strengthen me in virtue, whom I can legitimately call my own. On July 27, 1812, when she drove past me in Baden, she seemed to gaze at me."

"She" was Marie Koschak. It was an unhappy love. In 1816 he writes to Ries: —

"My kind regards to your wife. I, alas! have none. One, alone, I wished to possess but never shall I call her mine."

In this connection a statement made in the "Grenzboten," by Fraulein del Rio, of a conversation between her father and Beethoven, confirms the unhappiness of his attachment for the beautiful Marie. She writes: —

"My father's idea was that marriage alone could remedy the sad condition of Beethoven's household matters; so he asked him whether he knew any one, etc. Our long existing presentiment was then realized. His love was unfortunate. Five years ago he had become acquainted with a person with whom he would have esteemed it the highest felicity of his life to have entered into closer ties; but it was vain to think of it, being almost an impossibility, a chimera; and yet his feelings remained the same as on the very first day he had seen her. He added that never before had he found such harmony; but no declaration had ever been made, not being able to prevail upon himself to do so."

Marie Pachler and her husband were also friends of Franz Schubert, and to her he dedicated a number of his songs as a token of his esteem and friendship. It is touching to think that Beethoven, who had never made the acquaintance of Schubert, though living near him, did not really appreciate or recognize the beauty of his music until he was on his death-bed, when the songs dedicated to Marie were handed to him. He examined them, and exclaimed, " Truly, Schubert is animated by a spark of the sacred fire!" One year later Schubert passed away, almost his last words being the expression of a desire to be buried by the side of Beethoven. And now the world's greatest musician and Germany's greatest song-writer, strangers in life, sleep side by side.

There were two other attachments of Beethoven's which unquestionably exercised a strong influence upon his creative power. The first of these was for Bettina von Arnim, *née* Brentano, the wonderful child whom Goethe has immortalized no less than Beethoven. She it was who brought these two giants together. She keenly and thoroughly appreciated and understood the great master; and to her he explained, not only his own music, but all music, with an enthusiasm of manner, as well as closeness of analysis, that have never been excelled. One cannot read that extraordinary letter written by Bettina to Goethe, in which she prepares the way for a meeting between them, without feeling how closely Beethoven penetrated to the very soul of music, and how sacred his art was to him. The real meaning and character of music are better set forth in the few lines of this letter than in many volumes that have been written. Bettina, with a genius akin to that of Beethoven's, clearly comprehended him, and laid his very soul before Goethe with her glowing and enthusiastic eloquence, so that he was ready to embrace it, though the difference between the spiritual nature of the composer and the sensual nature of the poet was a radical one. Beethoven's attachment to Bettina was purely Platonic, and yet it was strong. His three celebrated letters to her furnish proofs of its strength, and equal proofs of the great influence she exerted upon him. On the 11th of August, 1810, he writes to her: —

"Art! Who comprehends it? With whom can I discuss this mighty goddess? How precious to me were the few days when we talked together, or, I should rather say, corresponded! I have carefully preserved the little notes with your clever, charming, most charming answers; so I have to thank my defective hearing for the greater part of our fugitive intercourse being written down. Since you left I have had some unhappy hours, — hours of the deepest gloom, when I could do nothing. I wandered for three hours in the Schönbrunn Allée after you left us; but no angel met me there to take possession of me as you did."

In 1811, about the time she was married, he writes: —

" I carried your letter about with me the whole summer, and it often made me feel very happy. Though I do not frequently write to you, and you never see me, still I write you letters by thousands in my thoughts. I can easily imagine what you feel at Berlin in witnessing all the noxious frivolity of the world's rabble, even had you not written it to me yourself. Such prating about art, and yet no results!"

In still another letter, written to her a year later, he bears direct testimony to her power over his musical creative ability: —

"Heavens! if I could have lived with you as *he* [Goethe] did, believe me, I should have produced far greater things. A musician is also a poet; he, too, can feel himself transported into a brighter world by a pair of fine eyes, where loftier spirits sport with him and impose heavy tasks upon him. What thoughts rushed into my mind when I first saw you in the observatory, during a refreshing May shower, so fertilizing to me also! The most beautiful themes stole from your eyes into my heart, which shall yet enchant the world when Beethoven no longer directs."

Elsewhere in the same letter he says : —

"Spirits may love one another, and I shall ever woo yours. Your approval is dearer to me than all else in the world."

The second attachment was for the beautiful Countess Guiletta Guiccardi, — one of his pupils, around whom popular fancies of all sorts have clustered, and several writers have woven very pretty romances. Mr. Thayer, in his biography, has done much to divest this attachment of its romance with his merciless dates and hard facts; but so long as it has probability on its side, and it has been believed for years without question, even as it was during his own life, let us still believe that she was the "Immortal Beloved" to whom he addressed such passionate letters, and of whom he writes to Wegeler : —

"I am leading a more agreeable and less misanthropic life. This change has been wrought by a lovely, fascinating girl who loves me, and whom I love. It is the first time I ever felt that marriage could make me happy. Unluckily, she is not in my rank in life; and indeed at this moment I can marry no one."

His feelings towards her admit of no question, as the following extract from one of the letters will show, which, Mr. Thayer to the contrary notwithstanding, we will assume was written to the Countess:—

"MY ANGEL, MY ALL, MY SELF,—A few words only to-day in pencil—your pencil [*mit Deinem*, the *Du* being used throughout the original]: only till to-morrow is my lodging fixed; what miserable waste of time! Why this deep grief when necessity speaks? Can our love exist except by sacrifice, by not demanding all? Can you help not being quite mine, I not quite yours? Ah, God! look into beautiful Nature, and calm your mind over what must be. Love demands all, and justly; so it is from me to you, from you to me; only you forget too often that I must live for myself and for you. If we were quite united, you would feel this grief no more than I. . . . My journey was terrible; I did not arrive till four in the morning: for want of sufficient horses the mail-coach chose a different route; and what a terrible road! At the last station they warned me not to travel at night, and frightened me with a wood; but that only tempted me, and I was wrong. The carriage could not but collapse in the terrible road, bottomless, a mere country road; but for my postilions I should have stuck there. . . . Now quickly from the external to the internal. We shall probably see one another soon; and to-day I cannot tell you the thoughts I had regarding my life during these few days. Were our hearts but always close together, I should have none such. My heart is full: I have much to say to you. Oh! there are moments when I find that language is nothing. Be cheerful; remain my faithful sole treasure, my all, as I am yours; the rest the gods must send, what shall be and must be.

Your faithful

LUDWIG.

Incoherent eloquence; but could there be a surer proof of love than its very incoherence? When Beethoven first knew the Countess, she was a lovely girl of seventeen, his pupil, and an excellent musician as well as a skilful linguist. She was possessed of every quality to attract him, — exquisite personal beauty, rare intellectual ability, irreproachable character, and withal was proud of his admiration, or rather adoration, of her. Beethoven then was twice her age; but disparity in years did not occur to him as an obstacle to their union, any more than disparity in rank, though he afterward discovered the effectual bar in the latter. There is every reason to believe that he offered her his hand, and that she would have accepted it had it not been for her father's opposition. She yielded to his remonstrances, and, at his solicitation, two years later married Count Gallenberg, an impresario and very prolific writer of very poor dance-music. The affair, therefore, was mortifying to Beethoven in a double sense, — first, that he should have been rejected at all; and, second, that he should have been rejected in favor of such an insignificant rival. It is said that upon her refusal he fled to the villa of her friend, the Countess Erdödy, then disappeared for two days, and was eventually found, exhausted with exposure and fasting, in a distant part of her grounds. Certain it is that he never entirely recovered from the pain and mortification of the rejection. He always spoke of her with tenderness; and nearly twenty years after, in a conversation with Schindler, alluded to his discomfiture with a sort of subdued bitterness. Of her influence upon him in his music there remains no question. If no other proof were at hand, the exquisite C sharp minor sonata, so familiarly known as the "Moonlight," which she inspired, and which he dedicated to her, would be sufficient testimony, in its wealth of beauty, tenderness, and passion, to the magic power of this woman's love over him. It is not unfair to assume that all he wrote during this period was made brighter, purer, and more majestic by her memory. Lost from his home and his heart, she shone resplendent in his music.

The instances I have cited — and to these many others might be added — show that Dr. Wegeler was correct when he said that Beethoven was always in love. Though fixed and grounded in every other habit of life, in love his nature was contradictory. In this long list of attachments there were but two that made a deep impression upon him. In the other cases he flitted from flower to flower, making butterfly pauses at each. His world was always an ideal one : ardent he may have been, but his passion was none the less austere. Surrounded with corruption, he led a life of absolute purity. Love to him was a light which illumines, not a flame that burns. He found more pleasure in the society of women than of men ; and if his energetic, impulsive nature suggested exaggerated feelings, it is very sure that they soon found their sentimental level in his cooler moments. His letters, which at first glance seem imbued with passion, when viewed from this stand-point are only expressions of aspiration rather than of desire. If there were no other proof of this, his purity and nobility of character forbid any doubt. If one wishes to know how these attachments affected him in his music, it is only necessary to look at the long list of his dedications, and remember that almost every one of them sprang from the relations of friendship and love. The very soul of Beethoven's music is love in its varying forms. His love for humanity rings out in the vocal finale of the Ninth Symphony : —

"Seid umschlungen Millionen
Diesen Kuss der ganzen Welt."

His love of freedom burns in the "Eroica." His love of God shines resplendent and majestic in the immortal measures of the Second Mass. His love of art is shown by the remorseless manner in which he pressed the thorns of life into his own heart, — this Titan doing battle with Fate, and winning immortality ; and all along the fields of this struggle are scattered the roses of woman's love.

FRANCIS JOSEPH HAYDN.

Sir, if you and I were both melted down together, we should not furnish materials for one Haydn. — MOZART.

"PAPA" HAYDN — not only the father of the symphony and quartet, but father to the musical world by the grace of his unaffected, naïve, fresh, and smoothly flowing numbers, so full of cheerfulness and good-nature — has been endeared to all musicians since his time by this familiar and affectionate prefix; but the homely family word is a strange misnomer when one considers his domestic relations and their influence upon his music.

Haydn commenced his musical career as a chorister in Vienna, having a voice of great power and beauty. In the midst of his success, however, as a vocalist, one disappointment after another overtook him; and, to crown all, he finally lost his voice, and was discharged from his position besides, upon some trivial pretence, to make room for another with greater vocal ability, and that other his own brother Michael. In his twentieth year he was thrown out upon the world without friends and without money, but, fortunately for him, with a very happy and hopeful temperament. He soon procured a few pupils, borrowed some money, rented a garret of an old stocking-weaver, — attracted by his sign, "A poor person can find a sleeping-room in the attic very cheap," — devoted himself to composition, made the acquaintance of musicians, and at last had the good luck to be selected as musical director and chamber composer to a Bohemian count. This yielded him a good salary for those days, and he thereupon began to think of marriage. He was of an excitable, impulsive temperament, and withal susceptible to female blandishments, and consequently was in a condition to accept whatever chance might throw in his way. The stocking-weaver had an only daughter, Mary, a young girl of lovely character and pious disposition, whose admiration of Haydn's musical talent soon developed into love for him.

There is little doubt but that the affection was reciprocated. Haydn was struggling at this time, however, between two strong passions, — love, on the one hand, and his mother's ardent desire that he should become a monk, on the other. The latter was the stronger; and he soon entered the Servite monastery as a novice, where he devoted himself to the pursuit of his art with the greatest industry. The stocking-weaver's daughter made no complaint when she found herself forgotten and saw that her love was hopeless. She died not long afterward; and among her last words to her parents were these: "Father and mother, you must pray for Joseph as long as you live; for he is a rare gift of God to men, and he will one day be a great man, but he will always remain humble. The world will applaud him, but he will not become unfaithful to his God on that account. He should not weep for me, but sing a hymn at night when he sits all alone at his instrument." Upon learning of her death, Haydn visited the parents, sympathized with them, and provided them with the money to procure her a befitting grave.

Haydn did not remain long in the monastery. He had not the monastic disposition, though he was a man of very simple and childlike piety. He could not seclude himself from a world in which he felt that he was destined to achieve a great name, nor abandon the profession of music, whose claims upon him were growing stronger and stronger. He was hardly out in the world again before another opportunity for marriage presented itself. Without any unnecessary delay he accepted it, and regretted it all the rest of his life. He was introduced into the family of a hair-dresser and wig-maker, named Keller, who was of a sufficiently musical turn to appreciate his talent. He had two daughters whose education was giving him much trouble, and was delighted when Haydn consented to give them musical instruction. The old wig-maker, having gained this point, took another step ahead, made the most desperate arguments to convince him he ought to love some one, and finally offered him the youngest daughter in marriage, who would have made him an excellent wife. Haydn, however, with the usual perversity of lovers, wanted the other, whereupon the disappointed younger sister retired to a convent. Not a whit discouraged, the wig-maker baited his hook with the other daughter, and easily caught the susceptible Haydn. Never was there a more ill-assorted match. The bride soon displayed herself as a scold and shrew of most ungovernable temper. She had no sympathy with his musical ambition, and no pride in his compositions. He himself said of her that she did not care whether he were an artist or a shoemaker. Long before the honeymoon was over, poor Haydn found himself tied to a Xanthippe, who when she was not utterly unsociable, which probably were his happiest moments, amused herself with curtain lectures of the most vigorous description. And yet, oddly enough, the termagant influenced his music in a very curious manner, and one not peculiarly agreeable to him. Added to all her other disagreeable qualities, she was a religious bigot and prude, with a decided *penchant* for entertaining priests and monks. She kept the house full of them; and they, realizing his genius, induced her to make him write sacred music. To the religious admonition and argument which she brought to bear upon him, she also added her own personal commands and objurgations; and Haydn, being already under good family discipline, could not do otherwise than submit; so, while the fat fathers were revelling below stairs in carnal enjoyments, " Papa " Haydn above stairs was writing anthems, motets, and masses for their convents and churches, for which he received no remuneration. One can easily imagine the wrath and imprecations he must have hurled at the prude and her roystering companions, as the sounds of their revelry smote upon his ears, and how little of the "Laus Deo" there was in his heart as his fingers penned the scores that were to be sung upon the following Sabbath. Gradually this kind of life became unendurable, and he sought elsewhere the happiness which he could not find at home. Fate, however, was kind to him, and brought him speedy release. The Capellmeister of the reigning prince, Paul Esterhazy, as devoted to music, even, as the present King of Bavaria, was growing old; and the Prince applied to Haydn to fill the position of second Capellmeister. Haydn joyfully accepted it, all the more so as it was an unwritten law of the musical Count that musicians' wives could not accompany them. It was a happy day for "Papa" Haydn. He not only secured a lucrative and important position, but, what was still better, a permanent release from domestic torture. It was a lasting separation from his wife; but he always acted honorably by granting her an annual stipend for her support. Whenever they met the meeting was sure to be a stormy one, and always on the subject of money. She was a spendthrift, and not only wasted half his earnings, which he always sent her, but contracted debts in his name, knowing he would pay them rather than have trouble. Year by year she grew more extravagant; but at last death put an end to her demands upon him. When the old Capellmeister died, he was appointed to his place, and had full control of the Prince's musical household, which consisted not only of an excellent orchestra, but also of a large chorus and corps of solo singers; so that he was enabled to bring out large works, and the symphonies and operas of his own composition. Besides these forces, he had travelling companies and *virtuosi*, and an elegant theatre, at his disposal. Musically he had everything that heart could wish; and in this musical atmosphere he composed nearly all his operas and most of his songs, besides some of his most important instrumental works. The place of his wife was very happily, but not very honorably, filled by Luigia Polzelli, a vocalist in the chapel, and wife of Anton Polzelli, a violinist in his orchestra. The lady was an Italian by birth, and an ordinary singer, but possessed of personal charms that commended her to him, and resulted in a *liaison*, at first very agreeable, but ultimately subjecting him to almost as much trouble as he had had with his wife, since the Roman woman made constant use of his violent passion for her to extort money from him. She had two children, one of whom was popularly supposed to be his son. There is no record that the Polzelli was of any benefit to him musically; certainly she was not morally.

There were those, however, who exercised a great and lasting influence upon his musical production; and among them was Madame Genzinger, the wife of a prominent physician in Vienna, at whose house he spent much of his time, and for whom he wrote several symphonies and a large number of sonatas. His correspondence with her was very voluminous; and it bears almost constant testimony to the powerful influence she exerted upon him, both during his service under Prince Esterhazy and after he had quit that service. Her husband was the physician in ordinary to that Prince, and it was thus he became acquainted with the family. He visited the house every

Sunday; and as the lady was a fine singer and an admirable musician, whose home was the centre of attraction for all the musicians in Vienna, he soon became an honored guest; and the acquaintance which was based upon music soon ripened into a lasting and honorable friendship, though the lady was by many years his senior. It is a bright spot to contemplate in the unhappy and not altogether blameless life of Haydn. Turn to almost any letter in their long correspondence, and it will be found to testify to her influence over him. At one time he writes: —

"I cannot but admire the trouble and patience you lavish on my poor talents; and allow me to assure you in return, that in my frequent evil moods nothing cheers me so much as the flattering conviction that I am kindly remembered by you."

At another time he writes: —

"Well, here I sit in my wilderness; forsaken like some poor orphan, almost without human society; melancholy, dwelling on the memory of past glorious days. Yes, past, alas! And who can tell when those happy hours may return, — those charming meetings where the whole circle have but one heart and one soul, — all those delightful musical evenings which can only be remembered and not described? Where are all those inspired moments?"

In the same letter he playfully laments the loss of the good things at Madame Genzinger's home, in the following humorously lugubrious strain : —

"I found everything at home in confusion. For three days I did not know whether I was *capell* master or *capell* servant; nothing could console me. My apartments were all in confusion; my pianoforte, that I formerly loved so dearly, was perverse and disobedient, and rather irritated than soothed me. I slept very little, and even my dreams persecuted me; for while asleep, I was under the pleasant delusion that I was listening to the opera of 'Le Nozze di Figaro,' when the blustering north-wind woke me, and almost blew my nightcap off my head. I lost twenty pounds in weight in three days; for the effects of my good fare in Vienna disappeared on the journey. 'Alas! alas!' thought I to myself, when forced to eat, at the restaurateur's, instead of capital beef a slice of a cow fifty years old; instead of a ragout with little balls of forced meat, an old sheep with yellow carrots; instead of a Bohemian pheasant, a tough grill; and instead of good and juicy oranges, Hungarian salad; instead of pastry, dry apple-fritters, and hazel-nuts, etc. 'Alas! alas!' thought I again to myself, 'would that I now had many a morsel that I despised in Vienna!' Here in Estoras, no one asks me, 'Would you like some chocolate, with milk or without? Will you take some coffee, with or without cream? What can I offer you, my good Haydn? Will you have vanilla ice or pineapple?' If I had only a piece of good Parmesan cheese, particularly in Lent, to enable me to swallow more easily the black dumplings and puffs! I gave our porter this very day a commission to send me a couple of pounds."

After Haydn had left Vienna and gone to London, under the management of Salomon, to give concerts, he continued his correspondence, and constantly expresses his obligations to her, besides sending her many of his compositions written expressly for her. During his London visit, where his concerts were all the rage, he made many female friends, — among them, Madame Bartolozzi, the wife of the celebrated engraver, for whom he wrote three piano trios and a sonata; the wife of John Hunter, a celebrated surgeon of that time, who wrote the words for many of his canzonets; Mrs. Hodges, whom he describes as "the loveliest woman I ever saw, and a fine piano-player," for whom he wrote many pieces; and, lastly, a lady named Schrolter, widow of the Queen's music-master, who conceived a violent passion for him, which was reciprocated, though he was then sixty years of age and she still older. Referring to her afterward, in connection with some of her letters to him, he said : "These are from an English widow who fell in love with me. She was a very attractive woman, and still handsome though over sixty; and had I been free, I should certainly have married her." For her he wrote three of his best trios. Of all his numerous female acquaintances, however, not one exercised such an influence upon him musically as Madame Genzinger, for whom his friendship was honorable. We owe much of his music to his wife; but the savage and truculent manner in which she inspired him was not conducive to the best work of his genius. To Madame Genzinger's exalted friendship and noble influence we must assign his best instrumental pieces; and who shall say that his two greatest works, the "Creation" and the "Seasons," written in his old age, when the passions had cooled and the dross of life had been swept away, when, as he himself says, "I knelt down every day, and prayed God to strengthen me for my work," may not also be attributable to the same inspiring influence?

WOLFGANG AMADEUS MOZART.

> He was a man whose mission in the world seems to have been entirely fulfilled; to whom it was given to link together the Godlike with humanity, the mortal with the immortal, — a man whose footprints not all the storms of time can ever efface, — a man who, amid all his lofty aims, esteemed the loftiest of all to be the elevation of humanity. — NOHL.

THERE were but two women who strongly influenced Mozart in his music, — his wife Constance and her sister Aloysia. When in Munich seeking the patronage of the Elector, and while yet a lad, he attended the German opera, and was much smitten with the voice and personal charms of Mlle. Keiserin, the *prima donna*, a *débutante*, who was singing in a work called " Das Fischer Mädchen," adapted from Piccini. It was only a boyish fancy, however, and resulted in nothing more serious than some gushing letters to his father about her; referring to which, several months later, he says, " I must confess that I was an ass to write such a complete falsehood." His heart was at one time lightly touched by his cousin Marianne, whom he visited at Augsburg; but it ended in a sportive mood between them, and, long after his departure, in many of his most rollicking, frolicsome letters, full of jest and banter, he alludes to it.

On the 30th of October, 1777, young Mozart arrived at Mannheim. The day after his arrival he visited at the house of M. Cannabich, the director of the Elector's orchestra. He went there many times afterward, for the director's daughter Rose became his pupil. She was a sprightly, beautiful, amiable girl; and a strong attachment sprang up between them, with music, however, rather than love, for its basis. Painters and poets afterward raved over her; but Mozart never was seriously touched except in admiration of her beauty, and by the strong musical sympathy between them, which led to his writing the B flat sonata for her, the *andante* movement of which he marked *amoroso*. It was a favorite movement with both. What story of passion it may have told her can be imagined. He at least never cared much for the response. His fate was yet to come, but it came very speedily.

About this time he made the acquaintance of M. Weber, an uncle of the composer of "Der Freischütz," who was a prompter and music-copyist. He was an honorable and open-hearted but poor man, with a wife and six children depending upon him for support. The second daughter, Aloysia, a girl of fifteen, had a remarkably beautiful voice, and Mozart offered to instruct her. The offer was accepted, and master and pupil soon became lover and mistress. His own letters tell the story of this ill-fated love so completely that we do not need to look elsewhere for it. On the 17th of January, 1778, he first speaks of her in a letter to his father, and says : —

"She sings admirably, and has a lovely, pure voice. She is only fifteen. She fails in nothing but in stage action; were it not for that, she might be the *prima donna* of any theatre. . . . My aria for ' De Amicis ' she sings to perfection, with all its tremendous passages."

Two weeks later he writes again, but only to inform his father that she had been singing with him at Kirchheim-Boland, the residence of the Princess of Orange. Meanwhile the two lovers are forming all kinds of impracticable plans, — among them, one to travel together. With that strong sense of filial duty which always characterized Mozart, he laid the plan before his father. He had never expressed even a suggestion of his love for Aloysia to him; but the father surmised it, and disapproved of the plan to travel. He now grows bolder in his letters, and makes no secret of his warm admiration of her, and strives also to induce his father to take an interest in her musical abilities. He wrote arias for her full of passion and feeling; and as she sang them to him with all the beauty and richness of her voice, there can be little doubt that the songs went to their hearts, and that they fully believed in the reality of their love for each other, never dreaming how soon the illusion would vanish. About the middle of March (1778) he went with his mother to Paris. The parting with Aloysia was a sad one: Weber wept, Aloysia wept; and Mozart writes his father: " Pray, forgive me, but really tears come to my eyes when I think of it;" from which we may infer that he himself also did a generous share of the weeping as he bade adieu to the Webers. In Paris, music occupied his attention; and concerts which he attended, and at which he played, tempered the sorrows of separation, and, we may well believe, allayed the rankling of the stings which his father's satirical allusions to his love-affair had left. Work is the universal panacea, but he by no means forgot Aloysia. He had in his mind the idea of a speedy marriage with her; and he writes to his father, July 31, intimating that he would like to leave Paris and return to Mannheim, where Aloysia was struggling against the cabals of jealous singers who were striving to prevent her from getting an engagement in the Court concerts at Munich. Little he dreamed of the fate that was to await him when he should see her again. Three months later Aloysia secured the coveted situation in that city; and Mozart immediately decided to seek an appointment there, that he might be near her. In December we find him in Munich, where he experienced the second painful shock of his life, the first being the death of his mother during their Paris visit. Aloysia was faithless to him. The blow came upon him like a thunder-stroke. She hardly recognized him when he met her; whereupon he went to the piano and sang a song of unconcern, with his heart full of tears. She had met an actor named Lange at the house of the Princess of Orange, was captivated with his appearance, and subsequently married him. Time was kind to the one, and cruel to the other. It healed Mozart's wounds, and brought him one who was the soul of honor and constancy. After Aloysia's marriage he could calmly write to his father : " I was a great fool about Madame Lange. I own it ; but what is a man not when he is in love?" The handsome actor whom Aloysia had married was a drunken, dissipated wretch, who went from bad to worse, until at last she had to separate from him. She continued her profession in Vienna, and in 1782 appeared in Mozart's " Die Entführung." Nohl says : —

" Neither happiness nor riches brightened Aloysia's path in life, nor the peace of mind arising from the consciousness of purity of heart. Not till she was an aged woman, and Mozart long dead, did she recognize what he really had been. She liked to talk about him and his friendship ; and in thus recalling the brightest memories of her youth some of that lovable charm seemed to revive that Mozart had imparted to her and to all with whom he had any intercourse."

There is every reason to believe that on the day Mozart lost Aloysia he gained her sister Constance ; because there is no question that the calm, quiet, domestic sister not only more thoroughly appreciated and understood him, but had long nourished a strong though unuttered love for him. She was the one whom he needed, the one whom fate had marked out for him. She was quiet and restful in temperament, domestic in nature, and patient, docile, and sweet in disposition. She was very fond of music; and though not possessed of the brilliant powers of her sister, she was still a singer of good taste and excellent voice, and had a deeper insight into music than Aloysia. Joined to a rare tact in managing household affairs, she had the influence necessary to assist and inspire him in composition. She first appears in his letters May 25, 1781, only a few months after the separation from Aloysia, who was now Madame Lange. She finishes a letter to his father, which business engagements had prevented him from closing, and only writes a few formal words regarding Mozart's concerts. On the 25th of July of the same year we find his first serious allusions to Constance, and these are not very encouraging. He writes to his father that he is going to leave the Webers because people are beginning to gossip. He says : —

"We went together twice to the Prater ; but her mother was with us, and as I chanced to be in the house I could not well refuse to accompany them; besides, at that time I had heard none of these foolish rumors. I must also tell you that I was only allowed to pay my own share: and the mother, having since then heard these reports from others as well as from myself, does not wish us to go anywhere together, and herself advised me to remove to another house in order to avoid any further unpleasantness. . . . I will not say that, living in the same house with the young lady to whom people have married me, I am ill-bred, and do not speak to her; but I am not in love with her. I banter and jest with her when time permits, but nothing more. If I were obliged to marry all those with whom I have jested, I should have at least two hundred wives."

Jesting saved him from one hundred and ninety-nine misfortunes, perhaps; but there was one whose strong, steady, deep love turned the edge of all his sportive jests, changed his frolicsome humor into serious feeling, and at last gave him home and happiness. How soon jest was turned into reality Mozart himself tells us; for in less than six months he writes to his father, announcing his love for her, and asking his consent to his marriage. The letter is an interesting one, as he draws a picture of his affianced : —

"But now who is the object of my love? Do not be startled, I entreat. Not one of the Webers, surely? Yes, one of the Webers, — not Josepha, not Sophie, but the third daughter, Constance. I never met with such diversity of disposition in any family. The eldest is idle, coarse, and deceitful, — crafty and cunning as a fox. Madame Lange (Aloysia) is false and unprincipled, and a coquette. The youngest is still too childish to have her character defined; she is merely a good-humored, frivolous girl, — may God guard her from temptation! The third, however, namely, my good and beloved Constance, is the martyr of the family, and probably on this very account the kindest-hearted, the cleverest, and, in short, the best of them all. She takes charge of the whole house, and yet does nothing right in their eyes. . . . Before releasing you from this subject I must make you better acquainted with the character of my Constance. She is not plain, but at the same time far from handsome. Her whole beauty consists in a pair of bright black eyes and a pretty figure. She is not witty, but has enough sound good sense to enable her to fulfil her duties as a wife and mother. It is utterly false that she is inclined to be extravagant; on the contrary, she is invariably very plainly dressed, — for the little her mother can spend on her children she gives to the two others, but to Constance nothing. It is true that her dress is always neat and nice, however simple; and she can herself make most of the things requisite for a young lady. She dresses her own hair, understands housekeeping, and has the best heart in the world. I love her with my whole soul, as she does me. Tell me if I could wish a better wife."

Surely here was a Cinderella in real life; but Cinderella and the Prince were to fight a hard battle yet, before they came to their own. The composer Peter Winter, while in Salzburg, filled the ears of Mozart's father with bad reports about his son and scandalous stories about Constance, and thus satisfied a grudge which he and his teacher, the Abbé Vogler, had against Mozart. The father replied to his son's letter in a furious manner; and the son was for a time hardly less indignant at the father for listening to such baseless accusations against him and his affianced, than he was at the slanderers. Constance's guardian (the father being dead) was also very uneasy at the insinuations against the young composer, and at last prevailed upon the mother to insist that Mozart should make a written contract of marriage. The contract was drawn up in this form : —

"I bind myself to marry Mlle. Constance Weber in the course of three years; and if it should so happen, which I consider impossible, that I change my mind, she shall be entitled to draw on me every year for three hundred florins."

Mozart, in a letter to his father, naïvely comments upon this contract:—

"Nothing in the world could be easier than to write this: for I knew that the payment of the three hundred florins never would be exacted, because I never could forsake her; and if, unhappily, I altered my views, I would only be too glad to get rid of her by paying the three hundred florins; and Constance, as I know her, would be too proud to let herself be sold in this way."

Constance had a more summary way of dealing with this contract. After the guardian had gone, she demanded it of her mother, and resolutely tore it to pieces, saying to her lover, "Dear Mozart, I require no written contract from you; I rely on your promises."

In January (1782) he again asks his father's consent, and is busy devising ways and means to procure money, first, for the performance of the marriage ceremony, and second, for support after marriage. He writes that he has in view three sources of income: first, the composition of music for a new military band about to be organized by Prince Lichtenstein;

second, the Emperor and the Archduke Maximilian; and, third, his pupils. More troubles begin to crowd in upon the luckless lovers. Malicious gossips are not only spreading stories about them, and Mozart's father giving ear to them, but Constance's mother, who all along has favored the alliance, now begins to grow indifferent to it, and demands that if they are united they shall stay with her; to which Constance is opposed, and Mozart, with a wholesome fear of mothers-in-law, decidedly objects. Indifference soon becomes irritation, and there is wrangling in the household, and the mother accosts the young lovers with sneering remarks. At last there is a quarrel even between Mozart and Constance over a petty matter; but it is only an April shower. The cloud passes quickly over, and the sun shines again; but the future mother-in-law remains cloudy with frequent storms, and at last the house becomes so hot that Constance quits it for the domicile of the Baroness Waldstädten, — a somewhat flighty, eccentric, and not altogether reputable person, but a good friend to them. This step precipitated the marriage. Madame Weber threatened to send the police to remove her daughter from the Baroness's house. Mozart and Constance decide to marry at once. He writes his father of his intentions; and the latter gives his consent, coupled with the condition, however, that he must expect nothing in future from him. His opera, " Die Entführung," had been performed, July 12, with great success, and secured him the means for the ceremony. They were married, August 4, in very simple style, at the house of the Baroness, four or five persons being present. Three days later Mozart writes his father : —

" Our sole wedding festivities consisted of a supper which Baroness Waldstädten gave us; and, indeed, it was more princely than baronial. My darling is now a hundred times more joyful at the idea of going to Salzburg; and I am willing to stake — ay, my very life, that you will rejoice still more in my happiness when you really know her, if indeed, in your estimation as in mine, a high-principled, honest, virtuous, and pleasing wife ought to make a man happy."

Eighteen years after Mozart's death, his widow married the Danish councillor, M. Nissen, and lived with him in Copenhagen; and her declining years were spent, in conjunction with her husband, in the preparation of the memoirs of the distinguished composer.

Notwithstanding many pinches of poverty and burdens of debt, their life together was a happy one. Their mutual love never decreased, but burned strong and clear to the end. She was his constant guide and monitor. She brightened all his days with her loving words and letters, and his love for her was always tender and delicate. She was a prudent manager of his domestic affairs, a safe counsellor in business matters, always a cheerful companion, and tended him in his last days with unfaltering devotion until the final bitter moment, when she flung herself upon his bed and prayed to die with him. The influence of Aloysia upon his music showed itself by the production of numerous brilliant arias which he wrote for her; but all his great works, "Die Entführung," "Idomeneo," "Don Giovanni," "Die Zauberflöte," "Nozze di Figaro," "Cosi fan Tutti," "Titus," the "Ave Verum," and the "Requiem," were written after his marriage; and every one of them bears, in greater or less degree, the imprint of Constance's influence. She took special care of his health, which was always delicate, so that his work might not be interrupted. She not only spurred him on to the fulfilment of his engagements; but when it happened that he was over-burdened with work, at which times he was apt to pursue his fancies late into the night to his physical detriment, she devised various means to relieve him. Her devotion to him in this regard was untiring. He immortalized her in the "Entführung," written when they were lovers. The main idea of the opera is based upon their relations to each other; and in it he pictures himself in the character of *Belmonte*, and her in that of *Constanza*. The Mass in C minor was written by him as a votive offering for her recovery in her first confinement, and she sung the solos at the first public performance. She was passionately fond of the Bach and Händel fugues, and never ceased her entreaties until he commenced writing in this form. The "Don Giovanni," "Zauberflöte," and "Requiem" are largely due to her. In his dedications her name does not appear as frequently as Aloysia's, for we only find six solfeggi, a fugue, two sonatas, and an aria written for her; but there was no need of specifying her name where almost everything was due to her love, her care, and her encouragement. In delicate health and straitened circumstances, the victim often of bitter musical jealousies, harassed by business complications, with which he was unfitted to contend, it is due to her, not only that he produced so much, but that his music preserved all its original joyousness, sweetness, and freshness, and that it has done so much to bless and gladden humanity.

FRANZ SCHUBERT.

Truly, Schubert is animated by a spark of the divine fire. — BEETHOVEN (*on his death-bed*).

FRANZ SCHUBERT, if not the creator, certainly the ablest and clearest exponent, of the German Lied, wrote from his inner life ; and his music, so full of beauty and melodiousness, only recently appreciated and known, will place him, in the near future, upon still loftier heights than he now occupies. The life out of which he wrote was in the main a sad one. There were days of cheer and gladness ; but the most of them were set to a minor key, so full of sadness and of suffering that they appeal to personal sympathy, though their experiences richly colored all he wrote. Exquisite as his songs are, they did not find a publisher until near his death,

and his best works were not known to the
world until long after the grave closed over
him; while even now there remain treasures
of his melody no voice has yet sung. Dwelling by the side of Beethoven, as he now sleeps
by his side, the latter never knew the worth of
his music until it was shown him on his death-
bed; and then he recognized "the divine
spark" of Schubert's genius. In all beauty
there is sadness. It is the test of beauty in
Nature, in humanity, and in music. It deter-
mines the motive of Beethoven's grandest
works. It colors with exquisite tints the
measures of Chopin, most poetic of all musicians. It is constantly present in Schubert's
works, though not one of them is morbid.
We may say that Schubert himself was morbid.
Certainly, sadness was almost the constant
habit of his life, dispelled now and then by
an excess of hilarity, which when it was ended
only left him sadder than before; but his
music does not reflect this organic morbid-
ness and despondency so much as it does the
effort to get out of the shadow into the sunshine. In this struggle he poured out the
rich treasures of his genius with marvellous
energy and industry. They reflect the beauty
of the sunlight, but the sun is always shining

through the cloud. Thus, in great degree the exponent of the common lot, his songs go to the heart, because they are full of the sorrows and the sympathies of the heart, tempering its joys. So long as there are voices to sing, the " Erl King," the " Wanderer," the " Ave Maria," the " Serenade," and the gems of the " Winterreise " will be sung, because they reflect the awful sadness of the supernatural, the pathos of the homeless, the piteous appeal of the soul to Heaven, and the sad and tender beauty of ideal love. It is a great genius singing by divine right out from the depths of his own sadness what is most sacred to every other heart. Search all through the long catalogue of his works, from song to symphony, and while you may find outbursts of joy, you will rarely find the triviality of humor; while you may discover the constant expression of sorrow and tenderness and pathos, there is no complaint.

The sadness of Schubert's life is more than once expressed in his letters and diary. In the latter (1816) he writes: —

" Man bears misfortune uncomplainingly, and for that reason feels it all the more acutely. For what purpose did God create in us these keen sympathies ? "

To his friend Kupelwieser, professor at the Kunstakademie in Vienna, he writes (1824):—

"Picture to yourself a man whose health can never be re-established, who from sheer despair makes matters worse instead of better, — picture to yourself, I say, a man whose most brilliant hopes have come to nothing, to whom the happiness of proffered love and friendship is but anguish, whose enthusiasm for the beautiful (an inspired feeling at least) threatens to vanish altogether, — and then ask yourself if such a condition does not represent a miserable and unhappy man."

And to this burst of grief he adds the hopeless words of Gretchen:—

"Meine Ruh' ist hin, mein Herz ist schwer:
Ich finde sie nimmer und nimmermehr."

How this sadness affected his music he more than once tells us. His diary says:—

"Grief sharpens the understanding, and strengthens the soul; whereas joy seldom troubles itself about the former, and makes the latter either effeminate or frivolous."

In his "Dream" he says:—

"For many, many long years I sang my Lieder. If I would fain sing of love, it turned to pain; if

I would sing of pain, it turned to love. Thus I was divided between love and sorrow."

Still more decidedly does he express himself in his diary (1824) : —

" My productions in music are the product of the understanding, and spring from my sorrow ; those only which are the product of pain seem to please the great world most."

Schubert had many sentimental friendships inspired of his music, but he was not an easy victim to love ; consequently his attachments were not at all serious, except in one instance to be alluded to hereafter, and that of so absurd a sort as to be almost incomprehensible, not the less so that it involved an abrupt transition from a *femme de chambre* to her mistress, a princess. He was susceptible to female charms, and had several alleged " affairs of the heart ; " but he said little about them and wrote still less. He was accustomed to make himself merry over the dolors of his friends who were in love, and is constantly bantering them in his letters and in his daily intercourse with them. It is questionable whether he ever seriously thought of marrying, though in his diary he once writes quite sentimentally : —

"Happy is he who finds a true friend; happier still is he who finds in his wife a true friend. To the free man at this time marriage is a frightful thought: he confounds it either with melancholy or low sensuality."

From this we may infer that if he had married it would have been in a Platonic sense. He was by no means proof against the tender passion, but it attacked him so lightly that he never compromised himself. He was not a stranger to deep and true affection, but physically he was not cast in a mould to be attractive to women. Had he been more fortunate in the latter regard, it is entirely probable that he might have married, and that, under happy domestic influences, much of the sorrow of his life might have been avoided. Nevertheless this man with a tender, loving soul, and a nature full of beautiful traits, set in an unattractive frame, had relations and friendships with the gentler sex which deeply influenced his music, though in the case to which I have referred they were as *bizarre* and inconsistent as could well be imagined.

One of the earliest of his compositions to attract public attention was his Mass in F, written for a festival of the parish church at

Lichtenthal, which he himself conducted. The soprano part was sung by Theresa Grob, a vocalist of considerable repute. Attracted by her voice and by the musical abilities of her brother, he had become at this time a frequent visitor at her home. Many of his masses and other compositions were rehearsed there, and several of his earlier songs were first sung by her in these musical gatherings. His interest in her, at first musical, soon became personal; but it never advanced beyond the limits of a romantic attachment, which was ended not long after by her very unromantic marriage to a baker. During his comparatively brief relations with the family he wrote a "Tantum Ergo" and "Salve Regina" for Theresa, and an adagio and rondo for her brother, who played with great skill, both upon the piano and 'cello. That he must have written many songs for her is also shown by the fact that the descendants of the Grob family still possess a large number of his compositions which have never been made public.

The great artist, Anna Milder, for whom Cherubini wrote the part of *Faniska*, and Beethoven that of *Leonora* in his "Fidelio," also played an important part in Schubert's musical productivity. She corresponded with him for several years ; and her letters are replete with valuable suggestions of themes for music, for which duty her long and varied experiences peculiarly adapted her, while she also made some of her most emphatic successes in singing his songs. Among other compositions written for her, was "Zuleika's Second Song," of which she says in a letter to him, "'Zuleika's Second Song' is divine, and each time I sing it my eyes fill with tears;" and the "Hirt auf dem Felsen," in which he departed from his usual Lied style by making the song of a bravura character to suit her dramatic method. She suggested to him many of Goethe's poems for music, gave him some very valuable advice about his opera "Alfonso and Estrella," and was the first singer to call special attention to his "Erl King," though she did not make such an immense success with it as Schröder-Devrient, who drew from Goethe the remark: "Executed as you execute it, the whole becomes a complete picture."

Marie Pachler, whose influence upon Beethoven we have already seen, also occupied a prominent place in Schubert's musical life. At the time he made the acquaintance of the Pachler family, it consisted of the husband,

Carl Pachler, Marie, and their son Faust. We have already seen, in the Beethoven chapter, that she was a lady of rare musical accomplishments and intellectual ability, and her home was the favorite rendezvous of composers and artists. In 1827 the family lived in Gratz, and in that year Beethoven had intended visiting them. He died about that time, however, and Schubert filled his place, going there with his friend Jenger, who was to have accompanied Beethoven. Many of his happiest days were spent in the charming society of this family. Many singers came and went. Excursions were made into the surrounding country. Little musical parties were given. Schubert sang his old Lieder, and wrote many new ones. Though at that time in the very valley of the shadow of death, they were the happiest days of his life. His visit is immortalized by numerous compositions. Belonging to those days are the songs, "Das Weinen," "Vor meiner Wiege," "Heimliches Lieben," and "Silvia," which are dedicated to Madame Pachler; the "Scotch Ballad," of Herder, written at her suggestion; the "Schluchtgesang," for double chorus; the "Ständchen," the "Nachtgesang im Wald" chorus, an Italian cantata, and many pieces of dance-music, among them the "Valses Nobles" and "Originaltänze." His music during this visit was of a very cheerful character; but immediately after his return home he composed the exquisitely beautiful but sorrowful cyclus of songs known as the Winterreise, in some of which it almost seems as if he recognized the shadows of the sad fate so swiftly approaching him.

Dr. Wegeler, in speaking of Beethoven's numerous attachments, says, in every man's life there is one complete love episode. Schubert is an exception to this rule. There was an episode in his life which he unquestionably thought was complete from an amatory point of view; though, to the practical, unromantic reader, it must have a serio-comic if not even a grotesque aspect. In 1818, then a young man of twenty-one, Schubert was recommended as a music-teacher to Count John Esterhazy. The latter, who was a princely patron of music, recognizing at once his abilities, proposed that he should enter his family, spending the winters with him in Vienna, and the summers at his country estates. It was an offer which Schubert gladly accepted. The Count had two daughters. — Caroline, then eleven years of age; and Marie, two years older. Both had excellent voices, the one soprano, and the other alto, and became his pupils. He soon was a favorite in the family, and was treated as an intimate. The atmosphere was a very musical one; but it speedily grew romantic also on Schubert's part, though no one else shared in his affairs of the heart. He first devoted himself to a flirtation with one of the servants, a *femme de chambre* to the Princess Caroline; to which at least we are indebted for the exquisite "Divertissement à la Hongroise," the themes of which are the Hungarian melodies he heard her humming as she went about her work. Finding that there was no response from the maid, he at once transferred his affections to the child Caroline; and notwithstanding the ridiculous disparity of age, the hopeless disparity in rank, and the general absurdity of the relation, his admiration of her developed into an earnest, fervent passion, which continued even to his death. The child was not too young to appreciate his genius, to admire his music, or to be sincerely attached to him as a friend; but she was too young, not only to reciprocate his passion, but even to conceive of it or understand it. She went on with her music enthusiastically, and was quite as enthusiastic in her admiration of the genius of poor Schubert; thus continually adding to the flame she had kindled in his heart without being aware of it. She always remained a good friend to him, and one of the most devoted admirers of his songs, as well as her sister Marie, who did all she could to assuage his pangs of heart when he found his passion was hopeless. She was not married until many years after his death. Some biographers declare the age of Caroline at this time to have been but seven years, which would make his attachment still more inexplicable. Leaving the affair of the heart, however, there is no question that the young Princess, as well as the whole family, exercised a powerful influence upon his musical work. He himself has left a record of Caroline's influence upon him; for upon one occasion, being reproached by her for not dedicating more of his music to her, he replied in the most abrupt and passionate manner, "What is the use of that, when everything I write belongs to you?" It was under her influence and that of her sister that he wrote the songs, "Abendlied," "Blondel zu Marien," "Ungeduld," "Des Müllers Blumen," "Erlafsee," "Sehnsucht," "Am Strom," and "Der Jüngling auf dem Hügel," the trio in E flat, two overtures for four hands, several waltzes, the "French Romance" in E minor, the Fantasie in F minor, the Variations (op. 35), and a piano duet (op. 140). All these works, besides many manuscripts not yet known to the public, are clearly attributable to the Esterhazy family.

Though Schubert never knew the happiness of love, he has sung of it with the purest ideal feeling. Though his life was clouded with sadness, he has given to the world immortal pictures in tones of the tenderest, loveliest, and truest aspirations of the heart. Though he died wretchedly poor in this world's goods, he bequeathed to the world a rich legacy, — the outpouring of a beautiful soul's musical wealth. The wastes of sorrow which stretch across his life were made beautiful with exquisite flowers of song, whose perfume will never be lost and whose beauty will never fade.

ROBERT SCHUMANN.

Beneath these flowers I dream, a silent chord. I cannot wake my own strings to music; but under the hands of those who comprehend me, I become an eloquent friend. Wanderer, ere thou goest, try me. The more trouble thou takest with me, the more lovely will be the tones with which I shall reward thee. — EUSEBIUS.

THERE was but one woman to whom Schumann was indebted for inspiration; and that was the woman who was the nearest and dearest to him of all women, his wife. Affianced to him by love and a kindred spirit in musical genius, she roused him to musical effort, she shared in his triumphs while he was living, and, from the day of his sad and untimely death until now, she has revealed the beauty of his music to the world. If he were a creator by the divine right of genius, by the same divine right she has been the interpreter. The bond of love and the affinity of music drew them together in an attachment nothing but death was strong enough to break. His name, his fame, his memory, she has preserved, and made still more beautiful by her own genius, and by the force and influence of her noble womanhood. Clara Schumann has kept her husband's laurels green, has placed wreaths of immortelles upon his grave, and has embalmed his name in an immortal love which had its birth in music, and which still knows no more beautiful or tender expression than in the revelation of that music to the world, though twenty-five years have gone since the poor crazed brain ceased its work.

Clara Wieck, daughter of Friedrich Wieck, the well-known teacher, who numbered such musicians as Schumann, Von Bülow, Krause, Spindler, and Merkel among his pupils, was born in Leipsic in 1819, and is still an honored and favorite artist in the concert-room. She commenced studying the piano with her father in her fifth year, and at nine years of age played in a public concert. Under her father's careful tuition, — and it is a thousand pities there are not more piano teachers like him, — she made slow but very sure progress.

It was no part of his method to hurry a pupil. How many teachers to-day can say with him: "I have always preferred a gradual, even a slow development, step by step, which often made no apparent progress, but which still proceeded with a certain constancy and with deliberation, and which was combined with dreamy sensibility and a musical instinct, requiring slow awakening, and even with a certain flightiness, one for which the patient labor and perseverance of six years or more was required, and where childishness allowed no encouragement to sordid speculations for the future"? In her eleventh year she also commenced the study of composition with Heinrich Dorn. Shortly after this she made a concert-tour to Berlin, Vienna, and other cities, which met with such success that it decided her to adopt the concert-stage, and enter upon the career of a professional artist. With this purpose in view she returned to Leipsic, and resumed her studies, which were very comprehensive in character, including technique, theory, harmony, counterpoint, instrumentation, score-reading, the voice, and the violin. The foundations of her future greatness as a *virtuoso* were laid deep and strong. For five years, from 1835 to 1840, she made concert-tours, which extended her reputation all over Germany and France; and during this period she did more than any other in making the German people acquainted with Chopin's music. All her associations and surroundings were calculated to aid her in her artistic career, and to prepare the way for just such a success as this remarkable woman has achieved in her long and honorable public life as an artist. She was not only trained with conscientious fidelity to the highest and noblest ideals of her art, but she was brought up in a musical atmosphere. At a very early age the great violinist Paganini was astonished at her precocity of talent, and when in Leipsic played with her almost continually. In Paris she heard Chopin, Liszt, Kalkbrenner, and other prominent artists; and many of their works she played for the first time in Germany. She had already commenced the work of composition; and in this connection a review of one of her pieces, the "Soirée für das Pianoforte," Op. 6, by Schumann himself, will be interesting. He says: —

"On one side this composition betrays such a tender and yet superabundant life that the most silent whisper could touch it, and again such riches of unusual wealth and fulness of intricacies and solutions as only the most experienced musicians could create. Where Sebastian Bach digged his golden treasures in the deepest shafts of his grand musical mines; where Beethoven, like a huge giant, flashes up toward the brightest regions of the skies; where the present masters bring forth their new combinations, endeavoring to reconcile the old and new, — all these unexplored regions are perfectly familiar to her, and yet she chats about them with the modesty of a maiden, and at the same time leads one to expect so much from her that one hardly knows where it all shall end. When you listen to the young artist's notes on the piano, interpreting her own innermost emotion, one cannot imagine how it is done. It seems almost impossible that such notes, such depths of feelings, can be written on paper with visible signs. In reality, one cannot express with words what she is. It is even impossible to describe the impressions her playing makes, not to speak of what she does to create such sensations."

There is something more than the mere critical spirit revealed in this eulogium. Read between the lines, it is not difficult to discover the human passion which inspired it.

When Schumann first met Clara Wieck, she was already recognized as a genius, though but a child. He was a musical student of a very romantic nature, exquisitely sensitive, moody even to the verge of melancholy, and completely permeated with the spirit of Jean Paul, whose works he had closely studied, and whose influence was already visible in his letters and other writings. It was during his visit to Leipsic in 1828 that he became acquainted with Friedrich Wieck. He formed a strong attachment for him; and the remarkable musical accomplishments of his daughter Clara led him to seek the same tuition that had developed such skill in her case. He requested Wieck to teach him; and the latter complied, though at this time he gave him but few lessons, and these were not satisfactory to his teacher, as Schumann kept himself within the narrow range of mere facility in playing, and, with the same persistence that characterized him for years afterward, declined to perfect himself in harmony. He never recognized its necessity until he commenced serious work for the orchestra, and then it was too late for him to reach his complete development. During all this time he had been studying law in deference to the wishes of his mother, who was bent upon making him a lawyer, while he was equally bent upon following music as a profession. At last, in 1830, he writes to her, desiring her to consult with Wieck, saying that he will abide by his decision whether he shall continue to study law, or return to Leipsic and resume his musical studies. His mother complies with his wish, and writes to Wieck : —

"All rests on your decision,— the peace of a loving mother, the whole happiness for life of a young and inexperienced man, who lives but in a higher sphere and will have nothing to do with practical life. I know that you love music. Do not let your feelings plead for Robert, but consider his years, his fortune, his powers, and his future."

Wieck had already considered his powers and his future during the short time he had taught him, and he replied at once in favor of Schumann's musical plans. The mother thereupon withdrew all opposition ; and the son enthusiastically writes to his old teacher, "Trust me, I will deserve the name of your scholar ; " and to his guardian, " I was born for music, and will remain true to it," — a promise never broken.

At Michaelmas, 1830, Schumann arrived at Leipsic, and resumed his studies. At the commencement of this chapter I have quoted from Wieck to show that he believed in the old maxim of hastening slowly. Schumann was impatient, and by over-practice in the prosecution of a system of his own devising, lost the use of his right hand. This ended his studies with Wieck, and his professional career as a pianist. He now entered upon the higher career of a composer; upon which Clara Wieck was to exercise a powerful influence, and also shone out speedily with remarkable brilliancy as a critic in the "Neue Zeitschrift für Musik," in the columns of which Florestan, Eusebius, Raro, and Serpentinus soon became as familiar as household names. Schumann entered upon his work with all the romance, zeal, fire, and freshness of youth. He heralded Chopin as the rising star in music, and first made him known by his criticisms, as Clara did afterward by her interpretations of his music. Jealousy was a thing unknown to him. He did more than any other to establish the fame, not only of Chopin, but of Franz, Heller, Gade, and Henselt, and was one of the first to recognize the genius of Berlioz, besides fighting a life-long battle for Schubert, Mendelssohn, and Hiller.

Up to this time Schumann's interest in Clara Wieck was purely of an artistic character; but even now she was influencing him, for in 1833 we find his "Impromptus" for piano upon a romanza which had been published by her. The theme was a favorite one with her, and he wrote eleven variations upon it; and the next year she appears in that picturesque and fanciful masquerade in notes, the "Carnival," under the pseudonyme of "Chiarina." In 1835 a sonata appeared "dedicated by Florestan and Eusebius to Clara." In 1836 his interest in Clara Wieck became not only artistic but personal. He fell deeply in love with her, and from that moment a struggle for her possession commenced. Of that struggle he writes, in 1839, to Heinrich Dorn : —

"There is much in my music, no doubt, that might seem like a narrative of the struggle for the possession of my Clara. You have probably been able to understand it. These very troubles have solely given the impulse to the 'Concerto,' the 'Sonata,' the 'Davidsbündlertänze,' the 'Kreisleriana,' and the 'Noveletten.'"

Up to 1840 Schumann had not written a single song; but after he found that she was really his own, no less than one hundred and thirty-eight of the most beautiful songs ever written attested his happiness. The father opposed their union, and it is doubtful whether his passion was at first returned. They were separated for some time by a concert-tour made by Clara and her father; but through a third party Schumann managed to hear from her, and to this party he writes, March 1, 1836: —

"Clara Wieck loves, and is loved. You might easily discover it by her gentle, almost heavenly look and mien. Pardon me if I omit for the present her lover's name. The happy pair met, saw, spoke, and became engaged, without her father's knowledge. He has discovered it, would cut it down, forbids all intercourse on pain of death; but they have braved him a thousand times. . . . Now comes my most heartfelt prayer that you will let me know all you can learn, directly or indirectly, concerning Clara, her feelings, and her life."

In 1837 he wrote to Wieck, asking for the hand of his daughter; and his answer may be inferred from the following extract from a letter written to his sister-in-law, Theresa: —

"The old man won't let Clara leave him yet; he's too fond of her. And he is really in the right; for he thinks we ought to earn more money first, so that we may live comfortably."

To attain that object he went to Vienna, but failed in his purpose; and he returned to Leipsic, and once more sought to mollify the obdurate heart of Wieck, who again refused his consent. He then appealed to the law; and in 1840 the Royal Court of Appeals requested the father to yield, which paved the way to their union. In September of that year he met her at Weimar at the house of a friend, and their nuptials were celebrated on the 12th of that month. In an extract already made from one of his letters, it is shown that the "Noveletten," the "Kinderscenen," and the "Kreisleriana" were inspired by Clara Wieck. It might be added that all his piano compositions from 1831 to 1840 — and they are very numerous — were born of his artistic and personal relations to her. Not only this, but she inspired all his lyrical work during the year 1840, which includes the songs already spoken of, revealing his inner life during this period. After their marriage the real work of his life began. He emancipated himself from the narrow limits of the piano, and commenced writing for the orchestra, both symphonies and chamber-music. It was the real work of his life; and the symphonies he has left, particularly the B flat major and the E flat major (the Rhenish), are eloquent suggestions of what he might have accomplished, following, as he did, closely in the footsteps of Beethoven, had not the derangement of his mental faculties brought his life to a tragic close.

Schumann had other attachments during his life, — among them, those for an amateur vocalist named Agnes Carus, whom he met in Zwickau, and whose singing had a rare fascination over him ; for Clara von Kurner, daughter of Dr. von Kurner, a chemist of Augsburg, of whom he writes to his friend Rosen, "The lovely Clara's image floats before me, both sleeping and waking ; " and with Ernestine von Fricken, who lived at Wieck's house in 1834, and studied the piano, whose blooming personal charms aroused his passion. To Henrietta Voigt, the wife of a Leipsic merchant, who was a very warm and influential friend of Schumann's in 1834, he writes in his Jean Paulish way : —

"I was completely exhausted yesterday, and your letter came. It soothed me like an angel's hand; that is, for a day and night, and this morning every nerve is a tear. . . . Is it a weakness to confess it ? 'T is my Ernestine whom I love beyond all measure ; 't is you, Henrietta, my beloved friend. You glorious creature, what can I offer in return for your supreme favor ? 'T is said that those who love each other shall meet again in some other star, where they shall live and rule alone. Let us hold this lovely saying to be true."

Schumann sought the fair Ernestine's hand in marriage, but his suit was unsuccessful. Not one of these attachments, however, specially influenced him in musical production. Clara Schumann was the genius of his life, the companion, friend, and counsellor of his work, the guide and inspirer that led him to his highest and most enduring efforts. Her ideal of art was always the purest and loftiest. As an artist she has commanded the homage and admiration of the world. As a woman she stands peerless in the nobility, dignity, and beauty of her womanhood. Since her husband's death she has been his faithful interpreter, besides editing his works. The love which crowned their lives with so much happiness, notwithstanding the cruelty of fate, still remains, and keeps the memory of the composer fresh by her executive tribute to his genius, and her loving and skilful interpretation of his works, which she did so much to inspire and help produce.

FELIX MENDELSSOHN BARTHOLDY.

Mendelssohn is betrothed, so is very much occupied, but great and good as ever. No day passes in which he does not utter at least two thoughts worthy to be graven in gold. — SCHUMANN.

NEARLY all the great and enduring music of the world has been conceived of sorrow or born in the struggle with destiny. The exercise of the heroic qualities in the battle of life has called out heroic music. Disappointments in life, the pressure of poverty, the pangs of suffering, the struggle against circumstances, and sometimes the spur of malicious competition, have aroused qualities of character in composers which have reflected themselves in their music. These elements have given us majesty, grandeur, and strength in music. More tranquil lives, kindly smiled upon by fate and lifted above all necessities, undisturbed by care and untouched by sorrow, have given us beautiful, graceful, elegant music, strains of enticing melody, and measures of smooth, flowing harmony, but rarely rising above the world. They may touch the heart, but they do not appeal to the soul. They may reveal the beauties of the earth and sky, but they do not go beyond finite boundaries, and give us glimpses of the infinite.

Felix Mendelssohn's music belongs to this class, and his life-currents ran in channels that were never vexed by a storm. Of all composers, it might almost be said of all men, his career and his experiences were the most fortunate. He belonged to a family remarkable for its talent in literature, philosophy, music, and the plastic arts. It was, moreover, a wealthy family; so that he not only had every advantage which wealth could procure in his studies, but during his entire life was enabled to surround himself with luxuries, and at no time was obliged to compose owing to financial straits. He was brought up in an atmosphere of art. The great poets, painters, composers, singers, and players of Europe were among the frequent and welcome visitors at his home fireside. He was endowed with rare personal beauty, and was richly gifted in scholarship and accomplishments of various kinds, as well as in those qualities of head and heart which attract a wide circle of friends and admirers. There was no sorrow in his life until his sister died, and then he succumbed to grief and soon passed away. The smooth and even tenor of his life had enervated him, as it were; and when the first blow came, it crushed him.

To estimate the influences of woman upon Mendelssohn's music, it is not necessary to go beyond the limits of his home circle; and these influences tended to color it with the same peculiarities of which we have spoken. His mother, his sister, and his wife — women of noble character, genial disposition, and loving nature — helped to impart to his music its peculiar grace and beauty. His mother first discovered his talent, and gave him his first lessons, and in his boyhood guided his studies, placed him under competent teachers, and accustomed him to hear the best music performed by the best musicians, with whom the Mendelssohn home was always a favorite resort. His sister Fanny, who afterward married the painter Hensel, was a pianist and composer of more than ordinary ability. In youth they were inseparable musical companions. They studied together; they composed together. Like her brother, she called about herself the best musical talent in Berlin. In the earlier collection of his songs, many of hers appear so closely similar in feeling and color that they would be indistinguishable were no signature attached. Devrient says : —

"His elder sister Fanny stood musically most related to him; through her excellent nature, clear sense, and rich fund of sensibility (not perceptible to every one), many things were made clear to him."

At the Sunday performances in the Mendelssohn home, she and her brother played in trios with a small orchestra which was accustomed to assemble there. His letters constantly bear testimony how eagerly he waited for her criticisms upon his work. Their musical sympathy was extraordinary, and is indicated by their correspondence upon more than one occasion in musical notation. Each was possessed of rare sensibility, and their musical affinities drew them together in a companionship of heart and soul which was never disturbed except by her sudden death. Devrient thus tells the sad story : —

"In perfect health and cheerfulness she had been presiding at a vocal rehearsal for the next of her Sunday performances on the afternoon of May the 14th (1847). All at once she felt her hands powerless at the keys, and was compelled to ask a friend to take her place at the instrument. The rehearsal proceeded. It was of the choruses of the 'Walpurgis Night.' She was listening to them from an inner room through the open doors, whilst she was fomenting her hands in hot vinegar. 'How beautifully it sounds!' she said joyfully. She thought herself restored, and was on the point of returning to the music-room when a second and total paralysis struck her; she lost consciousness, and had breathed her last by eleven o'clock that night. . . . Upon Felix her loss fell heavier than upon any one, bound up with her as he was in all his musical associations from earliest childhood."

Lampadius, in his "Life of Mendelssohn," says of her:—

"This cherished sister, Fanny, had been the companion of the great musician's pursuits during the years of childhood, in the days when they used to take five-minute lessons together, and in later days also, when (as I have heard him tell) they vied with each other which could best execute a certain difficult left-hand passage in Kalkbrenner's 'Effusio Musica.' Had Madame Hensel been a poor man's daughter, she must have become known to the world by the side of Madame Schumann and Madame Pleyel, as a female pianist of the very highest class. Like her brother, she had in her composition a touch of that Southern vivacity which is so rare among the Germans. More feminine than his, her playing bore a strong family resemblance to her brother's in its fire, neatness, and solidity. Like himself, too, she was as generally accomplished as she was specially gifted."

He never entirely recovered from the shock of her death. He secluded himself almost entirely within the family circle, and always seemed to be living in the presentiment of his own speedy departure. The last time that he had parted from her, she reproached him for not spending her birthday (November 8) with her. He replied, " Depend upon it, the next I shall spend with you." Fanny died May 14, 1847. He died November 4, the same year, and was with her upon her birthday. The influence of such a woman, bound to him by such strong ties of affection and such rare musical sympathy, cannot even be estimated. When she died, his hold upon music was gone. A few brief months, and they listened together to the music of a higher world, companions no more to be separated.

Mendelssohn's own home was full of the sunshine which had always illuminated his charmed life. Though a great favorite with women, and sought after by many, he had never contemplated marriage until the death of his father. The latter had always been anxious that his son should marry happily, and thus have the influences of a pleasant home surrounding him, and affecting his music. Only a few days after the funeral, knowing his father's wishes, he told his sister Fanny that he was resolved to marry. The event came speedily. In the summer of 1836 he was in Frankfort, conducting the Cecilia Society, and giving his "St. Paul" and some of the works of Händel. During his stay he had been introduced to the family of Madame Jeanrenaud, the widow of a minister of the French Reformed Church in that city. She was living with her children in her parents' home. The oldest daughter, Cecilia, at once attracted him. Devrient describes her as follows: —

"Cecilia was one of those sweet, womanly natures, whose gentle simplicity, whose mere presence, soothed and pleased. She was slight, with features of striking beauty and delicacy. Her hair was between brown and gold; but the transcendent lustre of her great blue eyes and the brilliant roses of her cheeks were sad harbingers of early death. She spoke little, and never with animation, in a low, soft voice. The friends of Felix had every reason to hope that his choice would secure repose to his restless spirit, and happy leisure for thought and work in his home."

And this was so, for never was there a happier home. The enthusiastic Élise Polko says of her : —

"Cecilia Jeanrenaud, whose mother belonged to a distinguished emigrant family, was at that period considered one of the most beautiful girls in Frankfort, always so rich in female charms, where indeed to this day, as in Saxony, 'fair maidens grow on every tree;' and when I now recall her image as I first saw her, though some time after her marriage, I feel that to this present hour she has always remained my beau ideal of womanly fascination and loveliness. Her figure was slight, of middle height, and rather drooping, like a flower heavy with dew; her luxuriant golden-brown hair fell in rich curls on her shoulders; her complexion was of transparent delicacy, her smile charming; and she had the most bewitching deep-blue eyes I ever beheld, with dark eyelashes and eyebrows."

Such was the fair vision that presented itself to Mendelssohn during his visits, which became more and more frequent and quickly resulted in betrothal and marriage. Of their courtship, Hiller, in his delightful "Reminiscences," says : —

"His visits became more and more frequent, but he always behaved with such reserve towards his chosen one, that, as she once laughingly told me, in her husband's presence, for several weeks she did not imagine herself to be the cause of Mendelssohn's visits, but thought he came for the sake of her mother, who, indeed, with her youthful vivacity, cleverness and refinement, chattering away in the purest Frankfort dialect, was extremely attractive. But though during this early time Felix spoke but little to Cecilia, when away from her he talked of her all the more. Lying on the sofa in my room after dinner, or taking long walks in the mild summer nights with Dr. S. and myself, he would rave about her charm, her grace, and her beauty. There was nothing overstrained in him, either in his life or in his art. He would pour out his heart about her in the most charmingly frank and artless way, often full of fun and gayety ; then again with deep feeling, but never with any exaggerated sentimentality or uncontrolled passion. It was easy to see what a serious thing it was ; for one could hardly get him to talk of anything which did not touch upon her more or less."

Their intercourse was one of the purest love. Their home was always a happy one, and the centre of attraction for all the great artists of his time. She was a good singer, was possessed of more than ordinary musical intelligence, sympathized with and encouraged him in his work, and rejoiced in his triumphs. She understood him, and she prized him at his real value. Slight as she was in physique, and calm and gentle as she was in her bearing, her spirit was more heroic than his. In all other regards she was his complement. She cared for him until his last moment, and strong in her very tenderness accepted his death with resignation and heroism. Of the funeral Devrient says, —

"When the church was almost deserted, a female form in deep mourning was led to the bier. She sank down beside it, and remained long in prayer. It was Cecilia, taking her last farewell of the earthly remains of Felix. She knew that she would not long survive him."

She lived but five years longer, and those years were lovingly and faithfully devoted to the care and education of his children. Then she passed quietly away, and, like her illustrious husband, was buried with imposing musical ceremonies.

The influences of mother, sister, and wife, all led Mendelssohn in the same direction of beauty and grace of style, rather than of great strength. His life never knew but one pang, and that was the last one. It was never clouded by any sorrows except such as are the common lot; and for these he had not the common endurance. It was a life without regrets and without reproach, and therefore a life without great moments or great struggles that call out the deepest and best that is in human effort. He imparted to his music his own elegance and grace; and it reflects also the gentleness, the sweetness, the loveliness, and the beauty of mother, sister, and wife.

FREDERICK CHOPIN.

Chopin died slowly, consuming himself in the flames of his own genius. . . . He was a poet of a mournful soul, full of reserve and complicated mystery, and familiar with the stern face of sorrow. He constantly reminded us of a convolvulus balancing its heaven-colored cup on an incredibly slight stem, the tissue of which is so like vapor that the slightest contact wounds and tears the misty corolla.— LISZT.

THE very name of Chopin suggests the name of woman, and of one woman more than any other, — George Sand. Liszt says his music is cannons buried in flowers. He himself was buried beneath an exterior of elegant *hauteur* and graceful courtesy, and no one ever penetrated to his inner self but the woman who was at once his good and evil genius. Under this goodly exterior was an imagination of exquisite fineness and power; feelings, though pent up, that raged at times like a volcano; a physical constitution enervated and undermined by disease; a pride so sensitive and so secretive that it allowed but one to intrude upon him or to peer into his inner life; a dread of human contact, not from hatred of men, but from the very fineness of his organization, that made him a stranger even among his friends. Such conflicting qualities of mind and body marked him out for suffering; but his suffering was concealed, as well as the real character of his life.

There is scarcely an event of Chopin's life, scarcely a phase of his passion or his temperament, hardly a phrase of his music, that is not related to woman. It was in his Paris salon, surrounded by lovely women, that he improvised so enchantingly. Almost every piece he has written was inspired of woman, and is dedicated to her. The finest interpreters of his music have been women. It was Clara Schumann who first really made Germany acquainted with it, as it was Robert Schumann who first proclaimed his genius in a critical manner. His passion itself was peculiarly feminine, as appears very clearly from his relations to George Sand. A woman's voice was the last sound he heard, as she sang in his dying chamber.

There are but two sources to which we can go for information that is authoritative as to the events of Chopin's life, and that bears directly upon the subject of woman's influence, — Liszt's so-called biography, which is in the nature of a rhapsody; and the biography recently written by M. Karasowsky, which may be considered reliable, though in some parts highly colored.

Liszt has drawn a fascinating picture of his earlier attachments, especially his love for a young lady who never ceased "to feel a reverential homage for him," but was lost to him by the more intense and fatal passion which George Sand kindled. Liszt says : —

"This young Polish lady, unfortunately separated from Chopin, remained faithful to his memory, to all that was left of him. She devoted herself to his parents. The father of Chopin would never suffer the portrait which she had drawn of him in the days of hope to be replaced by another, done by the hands of a far more skilful artist. We saw the pale cheeks of this melancholy woman glow like alabaster when a light shines through its snow, many years afterward, when, in gazing upon this picture, she met the eyes of his father."

At the house of the Princess Czetwertynska in Warsaw, a lady who was a passionate admirer of music, and who appreciated his playing and his talent of composition, he met with a group of young and noble ladies, — among them the Princess of Lowicz, the Countess Zamoyska, the Princess Radizwill, the Princess Jablonowska, and others, — who exercised a powerful influence upon him. Liszt bears testimony to this influence in the following glowing words : —

"As these visions of his youth deepened in the long perspective of memories, they gained in grace, in charm, in delight in his eyes, fascinating him to such an extent that no reality could destroy their secret power over his imagination, rendering his repugnance more and more unconquerable to that license of allurement, that brutal tyranny of caprice, that eagerness to drink the cup of fantasy to the very dregs, that stormy pursuit of all the changes and incongruities of life, which rule in the strange mode of life known as *La Bohême.*"

In 1830, at Nice, he met three beautiful and accomplished Polish ladies, Marie, Nathalie, and Delphine, daughters of Count Comar. They subsequently married wealthy noblemen ; and in their elegant Paris salons Chopin was a frequent visitor, and the centre of admiration and attraction. Their friendship for him was enthusiastic and lasting, and helped to inspire him to loftier effort than ever before; and one of them, Delphine, then the Countess Potocka, was with him in his dying moments, sustaining and glorifying them with her lovely voice.

His connection with George Sand cannot be called an episode. From the moment that he felt the weird fascination of this enchantress, he was completely in her power. She ruled his life. She changed its currents, directed its purposes, controlled its destiny, absorbed his very existence, until, in a fatal moment, he asked what it was impossible for her to grant; and then she left him, as one writer coolly says, "to his cough and his piano."

It were a difficult task to analyze the strange relations between George Sand and Chopin, because the two natures had little in common. The one was prosaic, virile, coarse, and unconventional; the other was poetical, feminine, delicate, and sensitive. They were allied in the possession of genius and in the recognition of what was beautiful; beyond this they touched at no point. The narratives of Liszt and Karasowski, so far as they cover this period of his life, though differing in view, for

Liszt himself had felt the influence of George Sand, are extremely interesting. Liszt draws an attractive picture of the coterie of poets and artists who were wont to assemble in Chopin's salon, among whom not one more clearly recognized his genius than George Sand. "After having named Madame Sand, whose energetic personality and electric genius inspired the frail and delicate organization of Chopin with an intensity of admiration which consumed him, as a wine too spirituous shatters the fragile vase, we cannot now call up other names from the dim limbus of the past," says Liszt. She was naturally anxious to establish a friendship with Chopin, for she shared with him his intense admiration of the beautiful; but he at first shrank from her, for his melancholy, sensitiveness, exclusiveness, tenderness, ideality, and sincere religious feeling were all repulsed by her boldness, energy, unconventionality, and masculine nature : but the acquaintance which she forced upon him at last dissipated all his fears ; and, as might be expected of such a nature, once devoted to an object, he concentrated himself with all the strength of that nature upon it, and was utterly absorbed by his ideal. Henceforth George Sand was to him a fatal necessity.

In 1836 his health began to decline. A year later he was seized with a dangerous illness, and was advised to go South, where he would have the benefit of a balmier climate. He selected the island of Majorca, and Madame Sand accompanied him. Under her care and the influences of the climate he improved. "He breathed there that air," says Liszt, "for which natures unsuited for the world, and never feeling themselves happy in it, long with such a painful homesickness." She herself says : —

"The funereal oppression which secretly undermined the spirit of Chopin, destroying and corroding all contentment, gradually vanished. He permitted the amiable character, the cheerful serenity of his friend, to chase sad thoughts and mournful presentiments away, and to breathe new force into his intellectual being."

For a time Chopin was happy, and Madame Sand was his inspiration. In her "Lucrezia Floriani," where he figures as Prince Karol, she says : —

"He was no longer upon the earth, he was in an empyrean of golden clouds and perfumes ; his imagination, so full of exquisite beauty, seemed engaged in a monologue with God himself; and if, upon the radiant prism in whose contemplation he forgot all else, the magic lantern of the outer world would ever cast its disturbing shadow, he felt deeply pained."

The dream, however, was suddenly dissipated. Liszt does not tell the cause, but it is well known. He desired her to marry him. His nature was all love. Love was his life. Madame Sand says : —

" He loved for the sake of loving. No amount of suffering was sufficient to discourage him. He could enter upon a new phase, that of woe ; but the phase of coldness he could never arrive at."

To transform a passionate friendship into a pure love was an impossible thing for her. They separated, and that separation strained and rent every cord that bound him to life. As Liszt says, —

" His last pleasure seemed to be the memory of the blasting of his last hope ; he treasured the bitter knowledge that under this fatal spell his life was ebbing fast away. He seemed to inhale the poison rapidly and eagerly, that he might thus shorten the time in which he would be forced to breathe it. Only a short time before he died, he wrote to a Polish friend : ' It is the end. I am only vegetating, and awaiting the last of it. I have never cursed any one, but now I am so worn and weary of life that I am now ready to curse that Lucrezia. But she suffers as well: ill-fortune devours her daily.'"

M. Karasowski's version differs somewhat from that of Liszt. According to the later biographer, chance brought him to Paris, and face to face with the woman who from that moment cast a dark and fatal shadow upon his life. One rainy day, in a fit of despondency, he travelled about the streets of Paris; and suddenly, remembering it was reception-day at a house where he was always a welcome guest, he turned his steps thither. As he mounted the stairs he fancied he was followed by a shadow from which there came a strong perfume of violets (his favorite flowers). He was about to retrace his steps, as if it were an ill-omen; but, smiling at his fears, entered the salon. He took his seat in a corner aside from the company, preferring to listen and be a spectator; but upon being pressed to play, he went to the piano and improvised. As he finished he became aware that a plainly dressed woman, leaning upon the other end of the piano, was gazing at him with a boldness and intensity that made him redden. A few minutes later she was introduced to him by Liszt as George Sand. His first feeling was aversion. In writing home about her, he says her features are coarse, and her voice harsh and masculine. She glowingly praised his playing, and each time she met him cunningly flattered him, until at last he was madly in love with her. Karasowski's narrative of their life in Majorca does not agree with Liszt's. According to the former, he was thoroughly uncomfortable and unhappy during the stay, and returned to Paris worse off in health than when he left. As his health declined, Madame Sand's passion for him cooled; and at last she found an occasion to quarrel with him, and he left her, vowing never to return. Some time after he met her at a friend's house. She held out her hand, and softly said " Frederick," as if she would be reconciled, but he turned away from her without recognition.

Sainte-Beuve has perhaps given the most reasonable explanation of the rupture between them. She felt a man's passion towards him, he felt a woman's love towards her; she was a woman of masculine nature, he was a man of feminine nature. When he proposed marriage her passion cooled, and she was ready to leave him as she had left others. His nature, being feminine, imposed upon him the female torture of endurance. Her attachment was in one sense a coarse one, to be ended at any moment by caprice or whim ; his was an absorption profound and unalterable : he was not necessary to her; she was necessary to him. It was a union of two natures with nothing in common, — most fatal of all mistakes. The cruelty of this relation was the first fascination ; a grotesque and unnecessary episode of it was the manner in which she has drawn his picture in the least attractive of all her works, " Lucrezia Floriani ; " the hopelessness of it was her refusal to marry, — a shock which his sensitive, affectionate nature could not sustain ; then followed the natural results to such a nature,— decline, despair, death.

His last hours were consoled and comforted by a tender, loving woman, who had been his friend and admirer before he came under the fatal influence of George Sand. Liszt touchingly and beautifully describes the scene : —

"On Sunday, the 15th of October (1849), his attacks were more violent and frequent, lasting for several hours in succession. He endured them with patience and great strength of mind. The Countess Delphine Potocka, who was present, was much distressed ; her tears were flowing fast, when he observed her standing at the foot of his bed, tall, slight, draped in white, resembling the beautiful angels created by the imagination of the most devout among the painters. Without doubt he supposed her to be a celestial apparition; and when the crisis left him a moment in repose, he requested her to sing. They deemed him at first seized with delirium, but he eagerly repeated his request. Who could have ventured to oppose his wish? The piano was rolled from his parlor to the door of his chamber, while, with sobs in her voice and tears streaming down her cheeks, his gifted countrywoman sang. Certainly this delightful voice had never before attained an expression so full of profound pathos. He seemed to suffer less as he listened. She sang that famous canticle to the Virgin which, it is said, once saved the life of Stradella. 'How beautiful it is!' he exclaimed. 'My God, how very beautiful! Again — again!' Though overwhelmed with emotion, the Countess had the noble courage to comply with the last wish of her friend, a compatriot; she again took a seat at the piano, and sang a hymn from Marcello. . . . The sacred silence was only broken by the voice of the Countess floating like a melody from heaven, above the sighs and sobs which formed its heavy and mournful earth-accompaniment."

Two days later he died; and his last act was in accordance with the love and courtesy which had always characterized him. He bent his head, and kissed the hand of his friend Gutman, and quietly fell into the dreamless sleep, leaving behind him a legacy of music, which, though small as compared with the works of other composers whom we have considered, is of imperishable beauty, and bears trace on every page of woman's love and influence, — trace, too, of woman's fatal spell, darkening and destroying.

CARL MARIA VON WEBER.

May God still grant me the blessing which he has hitherto so graciously accorded me, that I may have the power to make the dear one happy, and, as a brave artist, bring honor and advantage to my fatherland! Amen! — WEBER'S *Diary*.

FRIDOLIN VON WEBER, steward to the noble family of Schönau-Zella, grandfather of the composer of "Der Freischütz," had two sons. The elder became the father of Constance, the wife of Mozart; the younger, Franz Anton, the father of Carl Maria; so that the two eminent composers were cousins by marriage. Franz Anton's first wife was Maria Anna von Fumetti, daughter of the Court Financial Counsellor at Cologne, who died in 1783, worn out with the vagaries, eccentricities, and dissipations of her husband, who was a member of a strolling company of comedians. Two years afterward, being then in his fiftieth year, he married Genofeva von Brenner, a pretty girl of sixteen, who was destined to become the mother of Carl Maria. For years the child was carried by his patient, suffering mother in the company of the strolling comedians, surrounded by the worst of influences, and cared for, trained, and educated by her alone, until at last her health was shattered, and she fell into a decline. She died in 1798, and Franz Anton's sister Adelheid took the boy under her protection. She was a maiden lady of excellent judgment and kindly heart, and filled the mother's part in shielding him from the contaminations all about him, besides superintending his education. The influence of these two women upon the future of the child placed under such unfavorable circumstances was powerful for good, and unquestionably laid the foundations of his future fame.

In his eighteenth year Carl Maria, then earning a precarious living by teaching, made the acquaintance of Fraulein von Belonde, maid of honor to the Duchess Louise of Würtemberg, wife of Prince Eugene Friedrich, resident at Carlsruhe. She is described as an admirable piano-forte player. Impressed with the beauty of Weber's improvising, and sympathizing with his unfortunate circumstances, she became much interested in him and determined to aid him, and succeeded so well that she secured for him the position of musical director to the Prince, who not only took Weber himself, but his old worthless father and his good aunt Adelheid into his own house and kindly cared for them. Their stay, however, was not of long duration. The tide of war broke up their asylum. Weber drifted about for some time, almost hopelessly in debt and drowning his troubles in excesses of dissipation, until in 1807 he found himself in the service of Prince Ludwig and his wife, a princess of Nassau-Weilburg. He was intrusted with the musical education of their children; and, says his son in his excellent biography, "to this new position of the young composer are probably owing not only the 'six pièces à quatre mains' dedicated to the Princess Ludwig, but many others of his brilliant instrumental works belonging to this period." It was about this time that he wrote his opera "Sylvana" for King Friedrich's theatre, — an event which played an important part in his life, as it brought him in contact with Gretchen Lang, one of the singers, —

"the charming, winning, coquettish little serpent," with whom he became speedily fascinated. His biographer says:—

"She became the central point of all his life and aspirations. There is no evidence to show to what degree of intimacy this union of the two young fiery artist-natures was carried. It is certain, however, that from the time Carl Maria made Gretchen Lang's acquaintance, he seldom quitted her side."

It was an unfortunate attachment in every way. It brought down upon him the displeasure of his patron, secured for him the enmity of the King, and plunged him deeply into debt. Creditors pursued him, and at last he was sent to the debtors' prison. To crown his misfortunes came an order from the King that he should be transported beyond the boundaries of Würtemberg. In Frankfort he subsequently met Gretchen again, but her passion for him had cooled. He sought in vain to renew the old relations. They spent their last evening together at a concert, and in this moment of adieu to her he had loved so passionately he saw for the first time the one who was destined to be his wife. This was Caroline Brandt, who was the solo singer on the occasion. A few days later his opera

"Sylvana" was put in rehearsal. Gretchen was engaged at the theatre, but she refused to sing. The title rôle was given to Caroline Brandt, and it was due mainly to her efforts that the opera was successful. The composer was loudly called for at the close, and Caroline led him forward to receive the applause of the people. As his son says : —

"Little did the youth then know that the hand which clasped his was one day to be his own for life; that from that hand he was destined to receive his life's greatest happiness."

Many tribulations, however, were in store for Weber before he reached that important event in his life.

His prospects meanwhile were brightening. We next find him in Munich, with his new opera "Abu Hassan." Its rehearsals brought him in contact with the female artists and with a crowd of admirers who lavished their blandishments upon him. He passed a gay life among them; but the general result could not have been very favorable, for in his diary at this time he constantly writes : "All women are worthless," "All are bad alike." From a musical point of view, however, female influence added to his productivity and inspired his work. About this time he paid a visit to the Bavarian minister at Jegisdorf, and while there wrote his brilliant scena and aria from "Athalie," for the singer Frau Peyermann, an inmate of the house, to whose charms Weber was peculiarly susceptible. Had his visit been a prolonged one, the destiny of Caroline Brandt might have been disturbed ; for his next work for the singer was the " Künstler's Liebesforderung " ("The Artist's Declaration of Love "), one of the most beautiful of all his songs. Weber next appears in Prague as opera-director, busy with the rehearsals of Spontini's "Cortez." In the troupe was a dancer named Brunetti, who had been married for many years to a woman who had risen from the ballet to light operatic rôles. Weber's son says of her : —

" She was the mother of several children, but still possessed a considerable charm in her fine, plump figure, and her beautiful blue eyes. She was as full of the absurdest tricks and caprices as she was lively and impetuous in temperament; and that her reputation of being a mistress of all the finest arts of coquetry did not belie her, Weber had soon to learn to his cost. Thérèse Brunetti was fond of attending the operatic rehearsals, even when not herself employed. On these occasions Weber was frequently thrown in her way; and he soon conceived for the handsome, seductive woman a passion which seemed to have deprived his otherwise clear mind of all common sense and reason, and which neither the flood of administrative affairs nor the cold breath of duty could extinguish. Vain were all his efforts to conceal it. In a very short time it became the topic of general remark; excited the ridicule or grave anxieties of his friends; involved him in a thousand disagreeable positions; robbed him of the most precious treasures of a heart rich in love; lowered his moral character, without the slightest compensating advantage to his artistic career; and wellnigh dragged him down into an abyss beyond hope of rescue."

There is no doubt that Weber was thoroughly infatuated with this woman, and there is equally no doubt that she led him a life of torment. His diary is full of his troubles growing out of this relation, and lamentations over her unworthiness and his own folly; but still she kept him in slavery to her charms. His deliverance, however, was near at hand. Caroline Brandt arrived in Prague, and on the 1st of January, 1814, appeared on the stage under Weber's direction. I take the story of her *début* and what followed from his son's biography: —

"Caroline Brandt was small and plump in figure, with beautiful, expressive gray eyes and fair wavy hair, and a peculiar liveliness in all her movements. Her first appearance on the stage at Prague at once decided her position in that capital.

"The honor of a recall before the curtain — an honor in those days seldom bestowed — was awarded to her; and from the first, many of her competitors, among whom was naturally Thérèse Brunetti, began to look on her askance. This feeling of jealousy was soon increased. When introduced by Weber into the houses of Count Colowrat, Prince Lobkowitz, and others of the first families of Prague, she was welcomed there with the distinction due not only to her great artistic merits and her innate charms, but to the purity and worth of her moral character. Weber was thus thrown greatly in her company. He could not but feel the magic power of so fascinating a woman; he could not but draw comparisons, little by little, between the worthless object of his passion, — to whom, by a strange coincidence, Caroline Brandt bore a vague resemblance in fresher, younger form, — and this pure, bright, artless creature. Still, during the commencement of the year 1814 no traces are to be found of any diminution of his passion for the coquettish, artful Thérèse Brunetti. He suffered bitterly, it is true, from her deceptions, her sordidness, her infidelities ; but his heart yearned for love, and clung with desperation to the rotten plank on which he had stored all his hopes of requited affection. In the months of January and February there still appear in his note-book such remarks as, ' I was very sad ; but she was good to me, and I was content.' 'I found Calina with Thérèse, and I could scarce conceal the fearful rage that burned in me.' 'No joy without her, and yet with her only sorrow!'

"But the unworthy bond was at last to be broken; and the release was effected by two comparatively trifling circumstances. The tender lover, on the birthday of the object of his passion, had prepared for her a present, consisting of a gold watch, to which were appended a variety of trinkets, all chosen with symbolical reference to his deep affection. At the same time he had ordered her a dish of oysters, then a rare and costly delicacy in Prague. To the valuable watch the fair Thérèse paid little heed, still less to the profound meaning of the symbolical trinkets. She flung herself upon the oysters with a gluttony which disgusted the sentimental lover. On a sudden the scales fell from his eyes. The other circumstance was not perhaps so trifling. Weber had long remarked, with all the pangs of the most fearful jealousy, the marked attentions paid by Thérèse to a certain Calina, often alluded to in his notes, — a man of substance. Although this affair had become a matter of town talk and scandal, the infatuated adorer had still followed in the train of the delusive woman, until she herself announced to him, with the utmost coolness, that she had been offered, with her husband, an apartment in Calina's house, and had accepted it. This utter want of delicacy of feeling toward him revolted Weber. For once disdain overmastered passion. Still more irritated was he when he learned the foul advice given by Thérèse to Caroline Brandt, for whom the banker Kleinwächter showed a preference. 'Hold him fast,' had said the worldly-minded woman; 'he is worth the trouble, for he is rich.' All this might have failed in opening the eyes of a man so utterly blinded by mad passion, had he not had a little physician by his side, who had the best means of curing his disorder by the sweetest homœopathic medicaments, which doubtless had already begun to work their spell."

It was not long before his passion for Thérèse Brunetti was extinguished. Caroline charmed him more and more as he became acquainted with her; and at last he was allowed to pay his court to her, not, however, without rousing the demon of jealousy in Thérèse. She used every wile and fascination to gain him back. It was a long, hard struggle; but she failed. But now a fresh trouble arose; for Caroline was of a jealous disposition also, and the knowledge of his past relation to Thérèse, as well as the sight of her efforts to beguile him, very nearly ended the new love as well as the composer. Between the two charmers he was prostrated with trouble and bodily ailments, which had this good effect, however, that they removed him from the neighborhood of Thérèse's fascinations. By the advice of his friends he went to the baths of Friedland, and was thus released from the one tyrant and was able to devote himself more assiduously to the other. His ardent letters to Caroline soon smoothed over all difficulties, and removed her doubts of him for several weeks. They arose once more, however, before he returned to Prague, when she heard that he was again the centre of an admiring group. She tormented him with a letter on the subject, to which he answered : —

"Be pacified. The attention ladies show me is but the amusement or the affectation of the hour. There is no thought of love in it, my child. You must not suppose all other women have the same bad taste as you. The embraces of dear old Mamma Beer can surely be no reproach to me. My lips, eyes, and ears might all be subjected to the most inquisitorial examination."

Thus the two lovers were harassed by storm after storm. At last came a period of rest. Then scandal began to assail Caroline. She was charged with maintaining improper connections with Weber. To rescue her from this cowardly assault, he implored her to marry him at once. Acting upon the advice of her mother, she replied that she must have time to reflect whether she was ready to give up her art. Her answer led to a bitter quarrel between them, which was still further intensified by a fresh fit of jealousy on her part, owing to the alleged attentions which he had bestowed upon an actress named Christine Böhler, though there were no grounds for her suspicions. Overwhelmed with his troubles, he precipitately left Prague and went to Munich. During his stay in that city he received a letter from Caroline saying that it was best the engagement between them should be severed. He hurried back to Prague, and at their very first meeting the tie was renewed, never to be broken again; and with her consent public announcement was made of their formal engagement. From this moment his creative power reasserted itself, and song after song came from his pen, inspired by her love, while new positions of honor and distinction were offered him.

From this time also her influence is clearly apparent upon his musical work, particularly in his masterpiece, that flower of German operas, "Der Freischütz." He consulted her constantly, both in the preparation of the libretto and of the score; and her suggestions heightened its beauty and wonderful dramatic power. He called her his "public with two eyes," and when it was finished he said to her in a note : —

" The whole has now a far better effect, and I must thank you for that, my poppet. Your ideas were bold, but they have succeeded."

On the 4th of November, 1818, the fête-day of the affianced pair, they were married at Prague, and on that day he writes in his diary : —

" May God bless our union, and grant me power and strength to make my beloved Lina as happy and contented as my inmost heart would desire! May his mercy lead me in all my doings ! "

Though she was still occasionally harassed by jealous doubts of him when he was absent from her, their life was a very happy one.

In 1826, shattered in health, he left for London, whence he was destined never to return. As his wife heard the carriage door close, on the cold winter morning that he left home, she rushed to her room, sank upon her knees, and cried out in the bitterness of her soul, " It is his coffin I heard closed upon him." The only tie between them now was that of correspondence. His son says : —

"Nothing can be more touching than these letters, amounting in all to fifty-three, in which the sufferer was always striving to conceal, as far as he could, his sufferings; the anxious woman, left behind, always repressing her own bitter anguish lest it should increase the other's sorrow."

In another place his son says:—

"On the morning after the first representation of 'Oberon,' Weber lay exhausted in his easy-chair, when Fürstenau entered his room with a new potion. 'Go, go!' murmured the sufferer. 'No doctor's tinkering can help me now; the machine is shattered. But, ah! would but God in his mercy grant that it might hold together till I could embrace my Lina and my boys once more!'"

On the evening of the 2d of June he wrote his last letter to his wife:—

"What a joy, my own dear darling, your letter gave me! What a happiness to me to know that you are well! As this letter requires no answer, it will be a short one. What a comfort it is not to have to answer. . . . God bless you all, and keep you well. Oh! were I but amongst you all again! I kiss you with all my heart and soul, my dearest one. Preserve all your love for me, and think with pleasure on him who loves thee above all, thy Carl."

Two days later he called his friends about him, and with solemn earnestness turned to them and murmured, "God reward you all for your kind love to me." One by one they sorrowfully left the room. Fürstenau helped him to retire. He gave him his thanks, and then with a kindly smile illuminating his face said, "Now let me sleep." They were his last words. The next morning he was found dead. On the 14th of December, 1844, the body of the master reached Dresden, and was borne to the cemetery chapel amid thousands of people, who lined the streets and stood with uncovered heads paying silent homage to his memory. His son says : —

"In the richly decorated chapel of the cemetery, all the ladies of the theatre, with Schröder-Devrient at their head, awaited the body and covered the coffin with laurels. The ceremony was at an end. The torches were extinguished ; the crowd dispersed. But by the light of two candles still burning on the altar might be seen the form of a small, now middle-aged woman, who had flung herself upon the bier, whilst a pale young man knelt praying by her side."

The next day the body was placed in the family vault; and Richard Wagner, the rising genius of German music, spoke a solemn and eloquent tribute of praise over the remains of the composer of "Euryanthe," "Freischütz," and "Oberon."

RICHARD WAGNER.

I believe in God, Mozart, and Beethoven, and in their disciples and apostles. I believe in the Holy Ghost and the truth of Art, — one and indivisible. I believe that this art proceeds from God, and dwells in the hearts of all enlightened men. I believe that all may become blessed through this art. — WAGNER.

THE career of Richard Wagner, the musician of the future, the stanch protester against all that is artificial and conventional in music, poet, littérateur, and dramatist, the great high-priest who wedded music and poetry in a union now known the world over as the music-drama, was strongly influenced by the power of woman. His father, who was superintendent of police at Leipsic, died shortly after the composer's birth; and his mother, who, Dr. Nohl says, was "a woman of a very refined and spiritual nature," then married an actor,

Ludwig Geyer, who had been an intimate friend of the family. The step-father died before the boy had reached his seventh year, but he had already recognized his artistic talent and had intended he should be a portrait-painter. In his last sickness, however, he heard him playing melodies from " Der Freischütz " in an adjoining room, and exclaimed, " Can it be that he has a talent for music?" He commended him to his mother, and she did all in her power to realize almost the last words of her husband : " I would have made something out of him."

But little has been made known of Wagner's first wife, Minna Planer, an actress whom he married Nov. 24, 1836 ; but from that little it is certain that she was not a helpmate to him in any sense. She was an ordinary woman, having little knowledge of music and still less taste for it. She could not appreciate his ambitions, or understand the great purpose of his life. She died in 1866 ; but during her last years she had lived separately from him at Munich, supported by an allowance which he settled upon her. At this time Wagner was living in retirement at Triebscheu, near Lucerne, where Frau von Bülow, wife of the eminent pianist, Hans von Bülow, who keenly sympathized with his artistic aspirations, ministered to his domestic comforts. "This man, so completely controlled by his demon, should always have had at his side a high-minded, appreciative woman, a wife that would have understood the war that was constantly waged within him," is the judgment passed on his first wife by one of her own friends. This woman he found in Cosima von Bülow; and it certainly is an extraordinary tribute to Von Bülow's generosity, unselfishness, and self-sacrifice that he himself acknowledged the fitness of their union.

In 1834 Liszt, the pianist and composer, was the centre of a brilliant musical and literary coterie in Paris, which comprised such members as Chopin, George Sand, Lamartine, Victor Hugo, and others almost equally noted. Among them was the Countess d'Agoult, better known by her *nom de plume*, "Daniel Stern." His acquaintance with her ripened into an attachment of familiarity, which was at first attractive to Liszt and subsequently repugnant. He was considerably her junior, and she was already married; but she threw herself upon his protection, deserted her family, and became his travelling companion. She accompanied him in his years of travel through Italy and Germany, but in 1840 the attachment began to weaken. A short time before, he had written to a friend : —

" When the ideal form of a woman floats before your entranced soul, — a woman whose heaven-born charms bear no allurements for the senses, but only wing the soul to devotion, — if you see at her side a youth sincere and faithful in heart, weave these forms into a moving story of love, and give it the title, ' On the Shores of the Lake of Como.' "

The romance was a brief one. The Countess was speedily off to Paris again with her children, for during their attachment a son and two daughters had been born to them. The son, and one of the daughters, who married M. Émile Ollivier, the French statesman, are dead. The second daughter was Cosima, so named in memory of Como, who subsequently married Von Bülow. She was afterward divorced from him, and, as has already been said, met Wagner at Triebscheu. She was in complete sympathy with him, understood him, inspired him, and proved a blessing to him. They were married in 1870 ; and the first fruit of this union was the boy Siegfried, to whom the next year he dedicated the incomparably beautiful " Siegfried Idyl," which pictures the charming environments of his childhood at Lucerne. "For the first time in his life," says Dr. Nohl, "he secured that complete human happiness which sustains and animates our powers." Judith Gautier, in her charming volume, "Richard Wagner and his Poetical Work from Rienzi to Parsifal," gives the following pleasant picture of the family home : —

"At sunset I reached Triebscheu, that consecrated bit of land where since that time I have passed so many pleasant hours. It was a sort of promontory, extremely picturesque, jutting into the lake. There was neither grating nor door; the garden had no defined limits, and extended indefinitely toward the neighboring mountains. The exterior of the house was perfectly plain, — gray, with dark tiles; but in the interior arrangements, full of grace and elegance, one felt the presence of a woman. Madame Wagner appeared in the midst of her children, fair, tall, and gracious, with a charming smile, and tender, dreamy-blue eyes. The sympathy with which she inspired me from the first moment has never been broken; and our friendship, already of long standing, has never known a cloud. It was a delightful evening; the master displayed incomparable animation and gayety of spirits."

Never was there a more perfect companionship, perhaps, than that of Wagner and his wife. Whatever may be thought of the manner in which the separation from Von Bülow was accomplished, it was unquestionably in accordance with German law; and the fact that he made no objection to the separation, or to the subsequent union with Wagner, but on the other hand acknowledged its peculiar fitness, and that he was and still is one of the composer's stanchest and most zealous adherents, perhaps ought to satisfy the most scrupulous moralist. From the time that Wagner first met Cosima in Switzerland to the hour of his sudden death in Venice, his life was crowned with perfect happiness. She is a woman of rare personal accomplishments and extraordinary magnetic power, and she drew about her in their Villa Wahnfried a circle of friends and artists who made the atmosphere congenial and inspiring to Wagner. She herself, however, was the magician who exerted the most powerful influence upon him. She advised, consoled, encouraged, and inspired him. He lived always by her side, and he died in her arms, she not knowing that the beloved one had passed away, but fancying that he was asleep. After a life of strife such as few men have to encounter; of hatred more intense and love more devoted than usually falls to the lot of humanity; of restless energy, indomitable courage, passionate devotion to the loftiest standards of art, and unquestioning allegiance to the "God that dwelt within his breast," he rests quietly under the trees of Villa Wahnfried. Inspired by man's steadfast courage and a noble woman's love, he has lifted the musical art out of its grossness, artificiality, and vulgarity, invested it with a new body, and animated it with a new and pure spirit.

PART III.

WOMAN AS THE INTERPRETER OF MUSIC.

though inaudible to those standing around, kindles a smile upon the dying face, and brings a look of recognition to the eyes, as if they beheld once more the old familiar face of the mother, and heard the familiar voice which sung to the old man when all his world was contained in the hollow of a cradle? And between these extremes of birth and death in every age, what an endless procession of singers memory will summon! How they approach, pass before us, and disappear, crowned with their laurels of victory! The last two centuries have been prolific in great artists, though the present time is poorer than any other. To name only a few of them will suffice for the purposes of this essay; and they may readily and conveniently be divided into eras, as follows: From 1700 to 1750, the four great artists were Faustina Bordoni, Caterina Mingotti, Caterina Gabrielli, and Francesca Cuzzoni. Bordoni was from Venice, and Cuzzoni from Parma; and their names will always be associated in consequence of their bitter rivalry. Händel brought Bordoni to London to sing in his operas, in which Cuzzoni had already performed with success. Their simultaneous appearance was a signal for the most extraordinary popular demonstrations. The city was divided against itself; and the partisanship at last extended even to families, as we find Sir Robert Walpole declaring for Bordoni, while Lady Walpole was an enthusiastic advocate of Cuzzoni. The press was filled with stinging epigrams and atrocious libels. Duels were fought. The wrangling of audiences at times was riotous. One night, when the two queens of song appeared on the same stage, they came to blows. At last Bordoni drove her rival from the field, and the latter ended her days in a charity hospital. Bordoni continued her victorious career with great brilliancy for thirty years, winning in her last years the plaudits even of the captious critic, Frederick the Great. Her successor was Mingotti, a Neapolitan, who was educated by Porpora, and patronized by Metastasio. She eclipsed the fame of Bordoni, though her stage life was briefer. The last of the four, Gabrielli, who was educated by a cardinal of the same name, with the additional help of Metastasio, excelled all the others in natural talent, and aroused a frenzy of enthusiasm whenever she sang, with the brilliant execution and exquisite quality of her voice.

From 1750 to 1800 there were six representative singers : Gertrude Elizabeth Mara,

Sophie Arnould, Nancy Storace, Elizabeth Billington, and Angelica Catalani. Mara's name is inseparably connected with Händel's music. Insignificant in appearance and indifferent as an actress, her sweet and powerful voice and her unrivalled skill in bravura music more than atoned for her other deficiencies. When Frederick the Great first heard her sing, he testily declared he would rather hear his horse neigh; but she soon conquered the royal grumbler, and he speedily became her enthusiastic champion. In Paris she made a warm friend of Marie Antoinette. She brought all London to her feet by the manner in which she sang at the great Händel Commemoration in Westminster Abbey, in May, 1784. Burney, the musical historian and critic, who was present on that occasion, has left his impression of her singing, in the elegant volume he published, describing the various days' performances of that festival, which excelled all others held up to that time. Of her singing in the solo from Händel's anthem, " Oh, sing unto the Lord a new song," he says : —

" Madame Mara's voice and manner of singing in this plain and solemn air, so admirably accompanied on the hautbois by Fisher, had a sudden effect on myself, which I never before experienced, even from her performance of more pathetic music. I have long admired her voice and abilities in various styles of singing; but never imagined tenderness the peculiar characteristic of her performance; however, here, though she had but a few simple notes to deliver, they made me shiver, and I found it extremely difficult to avoid bursting into tears on hearing them. Indeed, she had not only the power of conveying to the remotest corner of this immense building the softest and most artificial inflections of her sweet and brilliant voice, but articulated every syllable of the words with such neatness, precision, and purity that it was rendered as audible and intelligible as it could possibly have been, in a small theatre, by mere declamation."

As an interpreter of sacred music this great artist stood almost peerless. Her triumphant career was continued to the extreme age of seventy-three; and on her eighty-second birthday Goethe dedicated a poetical tribute to her. Sophie Arnould was brought to Paris by Gluck, and sang in his operas under the patronage of Marie Antoinette with the most brilliant success. Nancy Storace was among the first who made successes in English opera. She had previously made a brilliant reputation in Italy, and carried Vienna by storm, including the Emperor Joseph, with whom she was a great pet. Elizabeth Billington, as beautiful in person as she was brilliant in song, captivated Haydn, during his London visit, with her beautiful voice. Sir Joshua Reynolds painted her as St. Cecilia, as a companion to his portrait of Siddons as the Tragic Muse. Haydn, contemplating the picture, exclaimed to the artist, "You have made a great mistake." "How! what!" said the startled painter. "Why," replied Haydn, "you have represented Mrs. Billington listening to the angels; you should have made the angels listening to her." Salomon, Haydn's manager, used to say, "She sings with her fingers," for she was a marvellous pianist as well as singer. Catalani had a career of almost unexampled success and good fortune, though a cold singer, carrying her audiences by storm with the tremendous volume and wonderful richness of her tone, as well as with the marvellous facility and rapidity of her execution. She had so powerful a voice that Queen Charlotte, after hearing her and being asked her opinion, declared: "I was wishing for a little cotton in my ears all the time." A wag, being asked if he would go to York to hear her, replied: "I shall hear her better where I am." A critic, describing her singing of Luther's Hymn, says: —

"The majesty of her sustained tones, — so rich, so ample as not only to fill but overflow the cathedral where I heard her, — the solemnity of her manner, and the St. Cecilia-like expression of her raised eyes and rapt countenance, produced a thrilling effect through the united medium of sight and hearing. Whoever has heard Catalani sing this, accompanied by Schmidt on the trumpet, has heard the utmost that music can do. Then in the succeeding chorus, when the same awful words, 'the trumpet sounds, the graves restore the dead which they contained before,' are repeated by the whole choral strength, her voice, piercing through the clang of instruments and the burst of other voices, is heard as distinctly as if it were alone! During the encore I found my way to the top of a tower on the outside of the cathedral, and could still distinguish her wonderful voice."

The half-century from 1800 to 1850 was rich in great artists; and to this period belong Pisaroni, Pasta, Schröder-Devrient, Anna Milder, Sontag, Malibran, Grisi, Falcon, Clara Novello, Pauline Viardot, Dorus-Gras, Persiani, Catharine Hayes, Alboni, and Jenny Lind, — a galaxy of singers unexcelled in all the annals of song. Meyerbeer and Rossini kept their pens busy for Pisaroni. Pasta, with her wonderful dramatic power, founded a new school of lyric art, and astonished the world with her personation of *Norma*, which Bellini wrote for her. Beethoven's *Leonora* in "Fidelio" will ever be associated with Milder, the creator of the part, — a singer of whom the aged Haydn said, when he heard her sing to her teacher, "The best way to form an idea of her voice is to hear a full, well-tuned organ register;" and of whom Napoleon more briefly said, "Voilà une voix!" Schröder-Devrient, the daughter of Sophie Schröder, described as "the Siddons of Germany," was also associated with this magnificent rôle, in which her success was extraordinary. Where have the great artists gone, that there are no longer any *Leonoras* or *Normas* of the heroic stamp? Of Malibran and Sontag, Théophile Gautier writes: —

"In 1827 Mlle. Sontag was attracted to Paris, the art-centre whither all celebrities tend. She made her *début* in the rôle of *Desdemona*. Her success was incredible; and it was no slight matter to occupy the *prima donna's* golden throne with Malibran, who was the most wonderful incarnation of music. Malibran, as great a tragedienne as a vocalist, — grace, self-possession, originality, poetry, and genius combined in one impassioned organization, — was reproduced by one of those rare miracles of which Nature is unfortunately too sparing. Their loyal rivalry was profitable to art; passion reigned on the stage and among the audience ; thunders of applause were evoked by both performers, for the two camps ended in uniting in a reciprocal enthusiasm ; Sontag's partisans applauded Malibran, and Malibran's partisans applauded Sontag. To gain access to the Italians, even by paying three times the usual price for a seat, was a rare favor; and the *queue* often included Meyerbeer, Halévy, Auber, Rossini. O happy days, when art engrossed all minds, and absorbed all political passions !"

Grisi was a peerless *diva* in personal beauty ; a great actress, especially in the rôles of *Norma* and *Lucrezia Borgia ;* and a singer who could act, as well as an actress who could sing, — a rare combination now-a-days. Chorley says of her : —

"A quarter of a century is a fair length of reign for any queen, — a brilliant one for an opera queen of these modern times, when wear and tear are so infinitely greater than they used to be. The supremacy of Madame Grisi has been prolonged by a combination of qualities rare at any period. In our day there has been no woman so beautiful, so liberally endowed with voice and with dramatic impulse as herself, Catalani excepted."

Mlle. Falcon, of the Grand Opera, achieved wonderful success as *Rachel* in Halévy's "Jewess." Says one who heard her : —

"Who does not know the power, the soul, which she threw into this glorious personation ? Who does not retain the strong recollection of her brilliant tragic and lyric qualities ? She was the genuine type of Hebrew beauty, — the real daughter of the Mounts of Sinai and of Bethlehem. The eagle eye sparkles with liquid flame ; the form of steel is pliant in its strength ; the complexion is brown and warm; the long hair of raven black floats in the breeze, free from that pale and sickly shade which the climates of the north give to the skins and locks of their daughters. It is ebony bathed in sunlight. When M. Scribe saw Mlle. Falcon, he perceived at once, with his usual penetration, that he had Judith before him, and that he had a glorious representative of a well-devised drama. That drama he wrote, and created for his heroine a world of tragic pomp, thrilling situations, and deep emotions."

Clara Novello, one of the noblest of women, commenced her career as an operatic singer, and closed it, with wonderful success, as the grandest oratorio singer England has yet produced, and the principal vocalist at the great English festivals. When Rossini first produced his "Stabat Mater," with Donizetti for conductor, she had the rare honor of being selected as the principal soloist. Persiani was one of the finest singers in the school of light operas, like "Lucia" and "Somnambula," and her *Rosina* in the "Barber of Seville" was always a triumph of enthusiasm. Pauline Viardot, second daughter of the famous singer and musician, Garcia, is still remembered for her wonderful personation of *Valentine* in "The Huguenots," and as one of those great dramatic singers of the grand school whose mantles are still waiting for successors. Schumann sang her praises; and M. Escudier, the great French critic, says of her : —

"Her singing is expressive, descriptive, thrilling, full, equal and just, brilliant and vibrating, especially in the medium and in the lower chords. Capable of every style of art, it is adapted to all the feelings of nature, but particularly to outbursts of grief, joy, or despair. The dramatic coloring which her voice imparts to the slightest shades of feeling and passion is a real phenomenon of vocalization which cannot be analyzed."

Madame Dorus-Gras, another great singer of this time, made almost as deep an impression in her personation of *Marguerite de Valois* in "The Huguenots," as Viardot in that of the principal rôle. Catharine Hayes, the lovely Irish singer; Bosio; D'Angri; Alboni, the greatest alto of the present century, whose sonorous and yet mellow liquid voice embraced fully two octaves, every note pure and beautiful; and Jenny Lind, whose fame is world-wide, — may almost be said to belong to the present day, so near are their victories to us. But who are their successors? The catalogue of singers in our own day is a long one; but, as compared with the list from 1800 to 1850, it does not contain equally great names. Two of the greatest singers of the present period, Tietjens and Parepa, are forever silent. Of all these artists, Tietjens was incomparably the greatest. One of the best of critics a few years ago wrote : —

"We presume it is useless to say a single word upon the extraordinary gifts and accomplishments of this truly extraordinary singer. A voice so rich in quality, so extensive and so flexible, combined with a temperament so passionate, and a dramatic perception so exact, carries us back to the highest standards of lyric excellence in our memory. The great line that commenced with Pasta, and was sustained in all its honors by Schröder, Malibran, and Grisi, finds no feeble vindication in the genius of Tietjens."

And with her the line stops. Madame Parepa-Rosa, "the stainless lady of the matchless voice," was a great vocalist, not a great *prima donna;* for she lacked the intense dramatic quality to make her personations complete and rounded. As a singer of exceptional power and beauty of voice, and as a versatile vocalist, she has rarely been excelled; for she shone with equal brilliancy in the opera, the oratorio, and in the ballad school, while in the beauty, sweetness, grace, and dignity of her noble womanhood, she commended herself to the public so intimately that her death was almost universally regarded as a personal loss. Zucchi, Lagrange, Gazzaniga, and Parodi were types of the old school, when great singers were great actors, and great actors were great singers; but they have retired, and we have left a list of beautiful, brilliant singers, nearly all of whom, however, have made their successes in the light works of the lyric stage, — Adelina Patti, Pauline Lucca, Marie Roze, Madame Torriani, Zelda Seguin, Emma Nevada, Emma Abbot, Alwina Valleria, Anna de Belocca, Minnie Hauck, Emma Albani, Christine Nilsson, Clara Louise Kellogg, Anne Louise Cary (lately retired from the stage), Etelka Gerster, Marie Marimon, and others; and on the concert stage Carlotta Patti, fast losing her brilliant powers, Miss Emma Thursby, Antoinette

Sterling, Mrs. Osgood, who has taken a leading position as an oratorio and ballad singer, Anna Drasdil, the veteran Anna Bishop, come down from a former generation, and a long list of others whom it is not necessary to mention. Will the Wagner school develop a second line of the heroic artists? It is not improbable; for already one has appeared, Frau Materna, the majestic *Brünnhilde* of the Nibelungen cyclus.

It is almost superfluous to emphasize the fact that the interpretation of vocal music is specially the province of woman, or that she is destined to achieve triumphs in the future as brilliant as those in the past. It is a realm where her sway will always be undisputed; and so long as there are artists to sing, they will inspire composers to write. It does not follow, however, that every singer will be a *prima donna*, though she may achieve a great name as an artist, and figure upon the bills and programmes by that appellation. Singers are plenty: *prime donne* are few. The late Richard Grant White, in one of his brilliant essays, "The Musical Monster," referring to Gabrielli, says: —

"No woman can be a great *prima donna* who has not to a certain degree her three principal qualifications, — a grand voice, the grand style which comes of fine and highly cultivated musical intelligence, and beauty, or, if not beauty, at least an attractive person and a pleasing manner."

Some exception might be taken to the last qualification, at least so far as he claims it to be an essential condition. Unquestionably personal beauty goes a great ways in making an artist a favorite with the public; but many artists with beautiful persons have been favorites with the public, who were not great *prime donne*, while many artists have been great *prime donne* to whom Nature had been unkind in the way of physical charm. Another qualification, and almost an indispensable one, should be added to his category; and that is repose, which is one of the foundation principles of true art. Still, while a given age may produce but few great *prime donne*, this should not be a discouragement, for it may produce many great singers who may give real pleasure to audiences. All composers cannot be Beethovens, any more than all painters Raphaels: but there are degrees of culture and service worth striving for by woman, that will command great success and ample reward; and no time was ever more advantageous for these results than the present. The conditions, however, are exacting. Any one can recall singers with exceptionally fine voices, who have failed, not because they had fine voices, but because they never had the patience, perseverance, and intelligence to learn how to use them. Duprez used to say, "Nothing injures a singer so much as a fine voice." Perhaps his aphorism would have been less exaggerated had he said, "Nothing is so fatal to a singer as to rely upon a naturally fine voice for success." The greatest singers have reached their positions by persevering study, resolute courage, patient endurance, and the constant habit of doing even the most unimportant thing well. A really great artist employs the resources of her art as conscientiously in a ballad as she would in a grand dramatic aria. With the proper study and a rightly directed culture, there is no reason why American women should not take leading places in the musical world, as they have exceptionally fine voices. Surely there is every impulse and incentive for study in the experiences of Adelina Patti, Emma Albani, Minnie Hauck, Marie Litta, Antoinette Sterling, Emma Osgood, Anne Louise Cary, Clara Louise Kellogg, and other American women who have made themselves famous all over Europe.

In instrumental music woman has not taken as high a position as in vocal music, mainly because her advantages have not been improved wisely. It has become the fashion to educate all girls, indiscriminately, to play the piano, without reference to their ability or musical taste. The result is that Clara Schumanns, Essépoffs, Mehligs, Goddards, and Krebbses do not abound, and that out of fifty young ladies who go through the conventional piano course, one may become a good amateur player. The gradus of the piano in our time seldom leads to Parnassus. There are other instruments which might be studied with great advantage by woman, especially the violin and harp. Camilla Urso, the sisters Milanollo, and Madame Neruda have shown what woman can accomplish with the violin. The instrument is admirably adapted to her delicacy of taste and sensibility, and nothing but a silly prejudice keeps her from its study. There is no reason why she should not learn to play, except it may be the awkwardness of the admixture of women in orchestras. This may militate against its study for such a purpose; but there is no reason why she should not strive to be a solo-player. The harp has gone out of fashion; but it should be speedily reinstated, not only as a beautiful medium of accompaniment and an elegant ornament for the drawing-room, but as the instrument above all others best calculated to display woman's taste and sweetness, and most happily adapted to her native grace of person and elegance of movement. The organ also should be more generally studied by woman, as a guide to a higher musical knowledge and the gateway to the truest and noblest forms of musical literature. Two women of this country — Miss Carrie T. Kingman of Chicago, and Mrs. Frohock of Boston — have shown that its most extreme difficulties can be mastered. The latter now devotes herself to the piano, but at one time took a high position as an organist; while the former, by constant practice and study, has mastered even the colossal difficulties of Thiele, and played the works of Bach, and the sonatas of Merkel, Haupt, and other modern German organ-writers, in a manner few male players can equal.

The instances which have been given in these pages are only a few out of the many, showing the influence of woman upon musical composers and in the field of vocal and instrumental music, which belongs of right to her, but which has not yet been cultivated with the earnestness and intelligence it deserves. Although not the creator, she has inspired the creations, and then interpreted them to the world. Man may be the intellect of music: she is its heart and soul. What she has not done *with* music matters little compared with the great glory and beauty she has given *to* music. By the side of the great composers, in equal glory and fame, should be placed such women as Constance Weber, Fanny Mendelssohn, Bettina von Arnim, Madame Voigt, the friend of Schumann, Cosima Wagner, Delphine Potocka, Clara Schumann, Pasta, Malibran, Grisi, and those others who have elevated music to greater heights by inspiring its creation, and giving it to the world through the medium of the voice.

No grander work can occupy woman's attention. Music was the first sound heard in the creation, when the morning stars sang together. It was the first sound heard at the birth of Christ, when the angels sang together above the plains of Bethlehem. It is the universal language, which appeals to the universal heart of mankind. It greets our entrance into this world, and solemnizes our departure. Its thrill pervades all Nature,— in the hum of the tiniest insect, in the tops of the wind-smitten pines, in the solemn diapason of the ocean. And there must come a time when it will be the only suggestion left of our human nature and the creation, since it alone, of all things on earth, is known in heaven. The human soul and music are alone eternal.

APPENDIX.

APPENDIX.

To make this essay complete, the writer appends, first, a list of the prominent female composers during the past three centuries; and, second, a list of the dedications made to women by the composers mentioned in the body of the work, so far as it has been possible to obtain them.

FEMALE COMPOSERS.

Seventeenth Century.

CACCINI, FRANCESCA. *Italy.* Songs.
CALEGARI, CORNELIA. *Italy.* Songs.
GUERRE, ELIZABETH CLAUDE. *France.* Operas.
STROZZI, BARBARA. *Italy.* Songs.

Eighteenth Century.

LEBRUN, FRANCESCA. *Germany.* Sonata for piano.
DUSSEK, SOPHIA. *Scotland.* Piano and harp music.
CIANCHETTINI, VERONICA. *Bohemia.* Concertos and sonatas.

AGNESI, MARIA TERESA. *Italy*. Operas.
ANNA AMALIA, *Duchess of Saxe Weimar*. Dramatic music.
ANNA AMALIA, *Princess of Prussia*. Cantatas.
PARADIES, MARIA THERESA. *Austria*. Operettas.
POUILLAU, Mlle. *France*. Three sonatas.
REICHARDT, JULIA. *Germany*. Songs.
SCHROETER, CORONA ELIZABETH. *Poland*. Songs.
SERNIEN, MADDALENA. *Italy*. Violin music.
WENSLEY, FRANCES FOSTER. *England*. Songs.
ABRAMS, Miss. *England*. Songs.
BAYER, Mlle. *Austria*. Songs.
BLANGINI, Mlle. *Italy*. Violin music.
BRANDENSTEIN, CHARLOTTE DE. *Germany*. Sonatas.
BRANDES, CHARLOTTE WILHELMINA. *Germany*. Songs and piano music.
BRESSON, Mlle. *France*. Songs.
GRETRY, LUCILE. *France*. Dramatic music.
GUENIN, Mlle. *France*. Operas.
LANNOY, LA COMTESSE. *Italy*. Romances and sonatas.
LILIEN, ANTOINETTE DE. *Austria*. Piano music.
LOUIS, Mme. *France*. Sonatas.
MARTINEZ, MARIANE. *Austria*. Masses.
MONTGERAULT, Mme. *France*. Sonatas.
TRAVANET, Mme. DE. *France*. Romances.
BLAHETKA, LEOPOLDINE. *Austria*. Songs.

Nineteenth Century.

MOUNSEY, ANN SHEPARD. *England*. Oratorio of "The Nativity"
MOUNSEY, ELIZABETH. *England*. Pieces for organ and piano.
LODER, KATE FANNY. *England*. One opera, one overture, and three sonatas.

LANG, JOSEPHINE. *Germany.* Songs.
HENSEL, FANNY CECILE. *Germany.* Songs and piano music.
GABRIEL, MARY ANN VIRGINIA. *England.* Operettas and songs.
BLAHETKA, LEOPOLDINE. *Austria.* Concert pieces for piano.
BONNE, D'ALPY. *France.* Songs.
CARADORI, ALLAN. *Italy.* Songs.
GAIL, SOPHIE. *France.* Dramatic music.
MILES, Mrs. *England.* Concertos.
BEARDSMORE, Mrs. *England.* Sonatas and songs.
SCHUMANN, CLARA. *Germany.* Songs and piano music.
DUFFERIN, COUNTESS OF. *England.* Songs.
POLKO, ÉLISE. *Germany.* Songs.
PUGET, LOUISE. *France.* Songs.
SAINTON-DOLBY, Mme. *England.* Songs.

DEDICATIONS.

MOZART.

Two sonatas for piano and violin, to Princess Victoire of France.
Two sonatas for piano and violin, to Countess de Tessè.
Six sonatas for piano and violin, to Queen Charlotte of England.
Six sonatas for piano and violin, to Princess Caroline of Nassau.
Aria, "Fra cento affanni," to Countess Firmian of Milan.

Two-act serenade, "Ascanio in Alba," to Maria Theresa.
Concerto for three pianos, to Countess Lodron and her daughters Aloysia and Giuseppa.
Concerto, to Countess Lützow.
Serenade, to Elizabeth Haffner.
Aria, "Ah! t'invola agli," to Josephine Duschek.
Aria, "Non so donde vienes," to Aloysia Weber.
Sonata for piano and violin, to Thérèse Pierron.
Six sonatas for piano and violin, to Princess Marie Elizabeth.
Song, "Oiseaux si tous," to Mlle. Wendling.
Aria, "Io non chiedo," to Aloysia Weber.
Aria, "Ah, non sò io," to Countess Baumgarten.
Aria, "Nehmt meinen Dank," to Aloysia Weber.
Solfeggien, to Constance Mozart.
Sonata for piano to Constance and Sophie.
Sonata for piano, to Constance Mozart.
Aria, "Ah! non sai, qual pena," to Aloysia Weber.
Aria, "Vorrei spiegar-vi," to Aloysia Weber.
Aria, "No, no, che non sei capace," to Aloysia Weber.
Mass (comp. 1783), to Constance Mozart.
Concerto, to Barbara Plöyer.
Sonata for piano and violin, to Regina Strinassacchi.
Trio, to Francisca von Jacquin.
Rondo, to Nancy Storace.
Aria, "Resta, O caras," to Josephine Duschek.
Aria, "Ah se in Ciel," to Aloysia Weber.
Aria, "Schon lacht der holde Frühling," to Mme. Hofer.
Aria, "Chi sa, chi sa, qual sia," to Mlle. Villeneuve.
Aria, "Vado ma Dove?" to Mlle. Villeneuve.

BEETHOVEN.

Sonata, op. 7, to Countess von Keglevics.
Three sonatas, op. 10, to Countess von Browne.
Trio in B major, op. 11, to Countess von Thun.
Two sonatas, op. 14, to Baroness de Braun.
First concerto, op. 15, to Princess Odescalchi.
Sonata in F major, op. 17, to Baroness de Braun.
Septet in E major, op. 20, to Empress Maria Theresa.
Sonata, op. 27, No. 1, to Princess Lichtenstein.
Sonata, op. 27, No. 2, to Countess Guicciardi.
Variations in F major, op. 34, to Princess Odescalchi.
Marches, op. 45, to Princess Esterhazy.
Rondo in G major, op. 51, No. 2, to Princess von Lichnowsky.
Aria, "Ah! perfido," op. 65, to Countess von Clary.
Trios in D and E major, op. 70, to Countess von Erdödy.
Six songs, op. 75, to Princess Kinsky.
Sonata, op. 78, to Countess Therese von Brunswick.
Three songs, op. 83, to Princess Kinsky.
Polonaise, op. 89, to Empress Elizabeth of Russia.
Song, "An die Hoffnung," to Princess Kinsky.
Sonata, op. 101, to Dorothea Ertmann.
Sonatas, op. 102, Nos. 1 and 2, to Countess von Erdödy.
Sonata, op. 109, to Fraulein Brentano.
Thirty-three variations, op. 120, to Frau Brentano
Twelve variations in F major, to Eleanore von Breuning.
Trio in B major (one movement), to Fraulein Brentano.
Twelve variations in G major, to Princess von Lichnowsky.
Six variations in D major, to Princesses Deym and Brunswick.

Lichte sonata in C major, to Eleanore von Breuning.
Nine variations in C minor, to Countess von Wolf-Metternich.
Twenty-four variations in D major, to Countess von Hatzfeld.
Twelve variations in A major, to Countess von Browne.
Ten variations in B major, to Countess Keglevich.
Eight variations in F major, to Countess von Browne.
Song, "An die Geliebte," to Regina Lang.
March in F major, to Empress of Austria.

SCHUBERT.

Three songs, op. 20, to Justina von Bruchmann.
Zuleika's Second Song, op. 31, to Anna Milder.
"Der zürnenden Diana," to Katharina von Lacsny.
"Nachtstück," to Katharina von Lacsny.
Seven songs from Scott's "Lady of the Lake," op. 52, to Countess of Wessenwolf.
"Divertissement à la Hongroise," to Katharina von Lacsny.
Overture to "Alphonso and Estrella," to Anne Honig.
Three songs, op. 92, to Josephine von Frank.
Four songs, op. 96, to Princess von Kinsky.
Fantasie, op. 103, to Countess Caroline Esterhazy.
Four songs, op. 106, to Marie Pachler.
"Der Hirt auf dem Felsen," op. 129, to Anna Milder.
Sonata in C major, op. 140, to Clara Wieck.

SCHUMANN.

Variations on name "Abegg," op. 1, to Countess d'Abegg.
"Papillons," op. 2, to Thérèse, Rosalie, and Émélie.
Impromptus, op. 5, to Clara Wieck.

Allegro, op. 8, to Baroness de Fricken.
Sonata No. 1, op. 11, to Clara Wieck.
"Fantasie Stücke," op. 12, to Anna R. Laidlav.
"Arabeske," op. 18, to Majorin Serre.
"Blumenstück," op. 19, to Majorin Serre.
"Humoreske," op. 20, to Julie von Webenau.
Sonata No. 1, op. 22, to Henrietta Voigt.
"Liederkreis," op. 24, to Pauline Garcia.
"Myrthen," op. 28, to Clara Wieck.
Three songs, op. 30, to Josephine B. Cavalcabo.
Three songs, op. 31, to Countess von Zedtwitz.
Scherzo, gigue, romance and fugue, op. 32, to Amalie Rieffel.
Six songs, op. 36, to Livia Frege.
Quintet, op. 44, to Clara Schumann.
Andante and variations, op. 46, to Harriet Parish.
"Dichterliebe," op. 48, to Wilhelmine Schröder-Devrient.
"Bilder aus Osten," op. 66, to Lida Bendemann.
"Waldscenen," op. 82, to Annette Preusser.
"Fantasie Stücke," op. 88, to Sophie Peterson.
Six songs, op. 89, to Jenny Lind.
Three songs, op. 95, to Cónstanze Jacobi.
"Bunte Blätter," op. 99, to Mary Poltz.
Six songs, op. 104, to Elizabeth Rutmann.
Six songs, op. 107, to Sophie Schloss.
"Jugend Album," op. 109, to Henrietta Reichmann.
Three "Fantasie Stücke," op. 111, to Princess Reuss-Kostritz.
Three sonatas, op. 118, to Julie, Élise, and Marie.
Three songs, op. 119, to Mathilde Hartmann.
"Albumblätter," op. 124, to Alma von Wasielewski.
Seven piano pieces, op. 126, to Rosalie Leser.
Five piano pieces, op. 133, to Bettina.
Overture to "Hermann and Dorothea," op. 136, to "Seiner lieben Clara."
Four songs, op. 142, to Livia Frege.

MENDELSSOHN.

Six vocal quartets, op. 59, to Henriette Bennecke.
Songs, op. 57, to Livia Frege.
Motets, op. 39, to the nuns of Trinita da Monti Rome.
Songs without words, op. 53, to Sophie Horsley.
Songs, op. 34, to Julie Jeanrenaud.
Songs without words, op. 67, to Sophie Rosen.
Concerto, op. 25, to Delphine von Schaurotte.
Songs, op. 47, to Constanze Schleinitz.
Songs without words, op. 62, to Clara Schumann.
Symphony (Third), to Queen Victoria.
Songs without words, op. 30, to Elisa von Worringen.
Songs without words, op. 38, to Rosa von Worringen.

CHOPIN.

Études, op. 25, to Countess d' Agoult.
Nocturnes, op. 27, to Countess d' Appony.
Polonaise, op. 44, to Princess de Beauvan.
Nocturnes, op. 32, to Baroness de Billing.
Valse, op. 64, No. 3, to Baroness Bronicka.
Rondo, op. 14, to Princess Czartoryska.
Scherzo, op. 54, to Mlle. Caraman.
Prelude, op. 45, to Princess Czernicheff.
Mazurkas, op. 63, to Countess Czosnowska.
Nocturnes, op. 48, to Mlle. Duperré.
Grande Polonaise, op. 22, to Baroness Est.
Allegro, op. 51, to Countess Esterhazy.
Bolero, op. 19, to Countess de Flahault.
Mazurkas, op. 17, to Mme. Freppa.
Scherzo, op. 31, to Countess Fürstenstein.
Berceuse, op. 57, to Mlle. Gavard.
Rondo, op. 16, to Mlle. Hartmann.
Valse, op. 18, to Mlle. Horsford.
Variations, op. 12, to Mlle. Horsford.

Nocturnes, op. 62, to Mlle. Köuneritz.
Rondo, op. 1, to Mme. de Linde.
Impromptu, op. 29, to Countess Loban.
Mazurkas, op. 56, to Mlle. Maberly.
Rondo, op. 5, to Countess Moriolles.
Mazurkas, op. 33, to Countess Mostowska.
Allegro de Concert, op. 46, to Mlle. Müller.
Ballade, op. 47, to Mlle. Noailles.
Sonata, op. 58, to Countess Perthius.
Nocturnes, op. 9, to Mme. Camille Pleyel.
Mazurkas, op. 6, to Countess Plater.
Concerto, op. 21, to Countess Potocka.
Valse, op. 64, No. 1, to Countess Potocka.
Valse, op. 64, No. 2, to Baroness Rothschild.
Ballad, op. 52, to Baroness Rothschild.
Fantasie, op. 49, to Princess Souzzo.
Nocturnes, op. 55, to Mlle. Stirling.
Barcarole, op. 60, to Baroness Stockhausen.
Polonaise Fantasie, op. 61, to Mme. Veyret.
Mazurkas, op. 30, to Princess of Würtemberg.

WEBER.

Two allemandes for piano, op. 4, to Mlle. Lisette d'Arnhard.
Variations for piano, op. 5, to the Empress Maria Theresa.
Variations for piano, op. 7, to the Queen of Westphalia.
Polonaise for piano, op. 21, to Margaret Lang.
Six pieces for piano, op. 10, to the Princesses Marie and Amélie of Würtemberg.
Recitative and rondo, op. 16, to Luise Frank.
Vocal duett, op. 31, to Queen Caroline of Bavaria.
Canzonet, op. 29, to Queen Caroline of Bavaria.
Six-voice song, to Madame Schröck.

Grand sonata for piano, op. 24, to the Grand Duchess Marie Paulowna.
Seven variations for piano, op. 28, to Fanny von Wiebeking.
Six waltzes, to the Empress Marie Louise.
Scene and aria, op. 52, to Therese Grünbaum.
Air Russe, op. 40, to the Grand Duchess Marie Paulowna.
Scene and aria, op. 51, to Hélène Harlas.
Cavatina for soprano, to Madame Weixelbaum.
Cantata "L'Accoglienza," to Maria Anna Carlina of Saxony.
Scene and aria, op. 56, to Mme. Milder-Hauptmann.
Mass in G, op. 76, to Queen Maria Amalia Augusta of Saxony.
"Invitation to the Dance," op. 65, to "his Caroline."
Concert-Stück, op. 79, to the Princess Marie August of Saxony.
Cantata, to the Duchess Marie Amalia of Saxony.
Cantata, to the Princess Therese of Saxony.
Song, "Nourmahal," to Miss Stevens.

INDEX.

Abbott, Emma, 199, 202.
Adelaide, 17, 61.
A bani, Emma, 199, 202.
Alboni, Mme., 193, 197, 198.
Arnim, Bettina von, 72, 205.
Arnould, Sophie, 190, 191.
Auber, 29, 195.
Bach, Johann Sebastian, 20, 129, 204; his ancestry, 35; youth and manhood, 37; his first wife, 38; her marriage and death, 39; his second wife, 41; their domestic life, 42; her musical influence, 43; Bach's death, 44.
Bach, Maria Barbara, 38.
Bartolozzi, Mme., 94.
Beethoven, 17, 20, 26, 28, 45, 60, 113, 118, 119–121, 135, 194, 201; domestic conditions, 62; the Breunings, 64–67; a flirtation, 67; Barbara Koch, 68; Mlle. de Gerardi, 69; Baroness von Drossdich, 69; Amelia de Sebald, 71; Bettina von Arnim, 72–78; Dorothea van Ertmann, 72; Magdalena Willmann, 73; Marie Koschak, 73–75; Countess Guicciardi, 78–81.
Belocca, Anna de, 199.

Berlioz, 20.
Billington, Elizabeth, 190–192.
Bishop, Anna, 200.
Bonheur, Rosa, 19.
Bordoni, Faustina, 188-189.
Brandt, Caroline, 165, 166, 168–176.
Breuning family, 64-68.
Bronté, Charlotte, 19.
Browning, Mrs., 19.
Brunetti, Thérèse, 167-171.
Cannabich, Rose, 97.
Caroline, Queen, 54.
Cary, Anne Louise, 199, 202.
Catalani, Angelica, 190, 192, 193.
Cherubini, 28.
Chopin, 17, 113, 128, 132, 179; a Polish attachment, 151; in Warsaw, 152; at Nice, 152; relations with George Sand, 153–159; his death, 159, 160.
Choral Symphony, 63, 83.
Cimarosa, 28.
Cuzzoni, Francesca, 188, 189.
Devrient, Edouard, 141.
Dorus-Gras, Mme., 193, 197.
Drasdil, Anna, 200.
Drossdich, Baroness von, 69.
Eliot, George, 19.
Erdödy, Countess, 81.

Eroica Symphony, 83.
Ertmann, Dorothea van, 72.
Essépoff, Mme., 203.
Esterhazy, 89, 91, 121-124.
Falcon, Mlle., 193, 195, 196.
Fidelio, 60, 118, 194.
Frohock, Mrs., 204.
Gabrielli, Caterina, 188,189,200.
Gazzaniga, Mme., 199.
Genzinger, Mme., 91-93, 95.
Gerster, Etelka, 199.
Glück, 28, 191.
Goddard, Arabella, 203.
Goethe, 72, 75, 76, 77, 119, 191.
Grisi, Giulietta, 193, 195, 205.
Grob, Theresa, 118.
Guiccardi, Countess, 78-81.
Händel, 20, 26, 28, 48, 110, 144, 188, 190; childhood, 49; his mother, 50; her death, 51; royal patronage, 52; queer matrimonial conditions, 53; Händel at court, 54; temper with singers,55; social habits, 56; relations with Vittoria, 57; anecdotes, 58.
Hauck, Minnie, 199, 202.
Haydn, Joseph, 17, 20, 28, 47, 84, 192, 194; his first love, 85, 86; courtship and marriage, 87; service with Prince Esterhazy, 89; an Italian liaison, 91; friendship with Mme. Genzinger, 92, 93; visit to London, 94; the English widow, 95.
Haydn, Michael, 85.
Hayes, Catharine, 193, 197.
Hensel, Fanny, 21, 140-143,205.
Herschel, Caroline, 19.
Honrath, Jeannette de, 67.
Hosmer, Harriet, 19.
Hummel, 28.
Jeanrenaud, Cecilia, 144-147.
Keiserin, Mlle., 96.
Kellogg, Clara Louise, 199, 202.

Kingman, Carrie T., 204.
Koch, Barbara, 68.
Koschak, Marie, 73.
Krebbs, Marie, 203.
Lagrange, Mme., 199.
Lang, Gretchen, 164, 165.
Lind, Jenny, 193, 198.
Liszt, Franz, 20, 128, 149, 151, 153, 155, 159, 179.
Litta, Marie, 202.
Lucca, Pauline, 199.
Lulli, 28.
Malibran, Mme., 193-195, 205.
Mara, Gertrude Elizabeth, 189-191.
Marimon, Marie, 199.
Materna, Frau, 200.
Mehlig, Anna, 203.
Mehul, 28.
Mendelssohn, 20, 29, 132; his sister, 140-143; descriptions of his wife, 144-147; his death, 147.
Meyerbeer, 29, 193, 195.
Milder, Anna, 118, 193, 194.
Mingotti, Caterina, 188, 189.
Moonlight Sonata, 17, 81.
Mozart, 17, 20, 26, 28, 65, 96, 162; his early fancies, 97: Aloysia Weber, 98; her sister Constance, 101; letter to his father, 104; a marriage contract, 105; love quarrels, 107; the marriage, 108.
Müller, Max, 24.
Neruda, Mme., 203.
Nevada, Emma, 199.
Nilsson, Christine, 199.
Novello, Clara, 193, 196.
Osgood, Emma A., 200, 202.
Pachler, Marie, 73-75, 119.
Parepa, Euphrosyne, 198, 199.
Parodi, Mme., 199.
Pasta, Mme., 193, 194, 205.
Patti, Adelina, 199, 202.
Patti, Carlotta, 199.

Persiani, Mme., 193.
Pisaroni, Mme., 193.
Potocka, Delphine, 152, 159, 160, 205.
Requiem, Mozart's, 17, 109, 110.
Rossini, 28, 193, 195, 196.
Roze, Marie, 199.
Sand, George, 17, 19, 149, 151, 153-159, 179.
Schubert, 20, 26, 28, 75, 112, 132; extracts from diary and letters, 114, 115; Theresa Grob, 118; songs for Anna Milder, 119; visit to the Pachlers, 120; the Esterhazy family, 121; relations to the daughters, 121-124.
Schumann, 20, 26, 28, 150, 195, 203; Clara Wieck, 126-137; other attachments, 136; marriage, 135.
Schumann, Clara, 21, 126-137, 143, 150, 203, 205.
Schröder-Devrient, Mme., 119, 176, 193, 194.
Schroiter, Mme., 94, 95.
Sebald, Amelia de, 71.
Seguin, Zelda, 199.
Somerville, Mary, 19.
Sontag, Henrietta, 193-195.
Sophie Charlotte, Electress, 52.
Staël, Mme. de, 19.
Sterling, Antoinette, 200, 202.
Storace, Nancy, 190, 191.

Thursby, Emma, 199.
Tietjens, Theresa, 198.
Torriani, Mme., 199.
Trouveresses, 21.
Urso, Camilla, 203.
Valleria, Alwina, 199.
Verdi, 28.
Viardot, Pauline, 193, 197.
Vittoria, 57.
Vogler, 105.
Voigt, Henrietta, 136, 205.
Von Bülow, 178, 182.
Wagner, 20, 26, 28, 176, 200; his youth, 177; his first wife, 178; meeting with Cosima von Bülow, 178; the second marriage, 180; his death, 182.
Wagner, Cosima, 178, 180-183, 205.
Weber, 17, 28; his ancestry, 162; meeting with Gretchen Lang, 164; Caroline Brandt, 165; troubles with Brunetti, 167; engagement to Caroline Brandt, 173; marriage, 174; his death, 176.
Weber, Aloysia, 96, 98-102, 109.
Weber, Constance, 101-110, 162, 205.
Wegeler, 63, 64, 68, 78, 82, 121.
Willmann, Magdalena, 73.
Wülkens, Anna Magdalena, 41.
Zucchi, Mme., 199.

www.ingramcontent.com/pod-product-compliance
Lightning Source LLC
Chambersburg PA
CBHW020933230426
43666CB00008B/1661